A POWERFUL CULTURE
STARTS WITH YOU

Cultivate a Thriving Workplace from the Inside Out

SHAHRZAD NOORAVI, PSYD, MCC

Publisher's Cataloging-in-Publication data
Names: Nooravi, Shahrzad, author.
Title: A powerful culture starts with you : cultivate a thriving workplace from the
inside out / Shahrzad Nooravi, PSYD, MCC.
Description: Includes bibliographical references. | La Jolla, CA: Strategy Meets
Performance Inc., 2022.
Identifiers: LCCN: 2022906658 | ISBN: 979-8-9856867-1-5 (hardcover) | 979-
8-9856867-0-8 (paperback) | 979-8-9856867-2-2 (ebook) | 979-8-9856867-3-9
(audio)
Subjects: LCSH Leadership. | Corporate culture. | Organizational behavior.
| Organizational effectiveness. | Success in business. | BISAC BUSINESS &
ECONOMICS / Leadership | BUSINESS & ECONOMICS / Human Resources &
Personnel Management | BUSINESS & ECONOMICS / Organizational Behavior
| BUSINESS & ECONOMICS / Workplace Culture
Classification: LCC HD58.7 .N66 2022 | DDC 658.4--dc23

PRAISE FOR
A POWERFUL CULTURE STARTS WITH YOU

A Powerful Culture Starts with You is just the book we need right now to help leaders create energized, engaging environments where people can thrive. Inspired people take care of their customers, which in turn drives business and leads to a healthy bottom line. But it all starts with you, so read this book and apply its wisdom!

> —**Ken Blanchard,** coauthor of *The New One Minute Manager®* and *Simple Truths of Leadership*

Dr. Nooravi has brought together principles of organizational development, team dynamics, change management and coaching into a compelling culture guide. The tools for examining culture, coaching and alignment of the senior team are practical and actionable. I recommend *A Powerful Culture Starts with You* for leaders ready to evolve their leadership and culture to meet the unique challenges of today's world.

> —**Pamela McLean,** PhD, Co-Founder & Chief Knowledge Officer, Hudson Institute of Coaching, author of *Self as Coach, Self as Leader* and *Completely Revised Handbook of Coaching*

Though it is widely believed that culture change can come from anywhere in an organization, this book argues quite clearly that unless the executive suite and the CEO are deeply involved as originators, supporters, and implementers of cultural evolution, it will at best only create minor behavioral changes that won't last. An organization's culture can only be an advantage if it is owned, implemented and illustrated by the leaders' own behaviors. This book is full of useful and practical ideas of when and how to create and manage workplace culture.

> —**Edgar H. Schein,** Professor Emeritus, MIT Sloan School of Management, author with Peter Schein of *Organizational Culture and Leadership,* 5th ed. *(2017)* and *The Corporate Culture Survival Guide,* 3rd ed. *(2019)*

A *Powerful Culture Starts with You* provides a practical approach for how leaders can transform a company's culture. The models in the book provide easy-to-use guidelines that any leader can learn from in order to create positive, sustainable culture change.

—**Tamie Zrecny,** Global Learning Lead, Microsoft

Dr. Nooravi has created a playbook for creating a strong workplace. As a colleague with similar training, I know that these models and techniques work. I encourage leaders to enjoy and learn from the many engaging case studies in this book. You may see yourself and your team members in these real-life examples.

—**Damian Goldvarg,** PhD, MCC, CSP, ESIA, author of
Professional Coaching Competencies: The Complete Guide, Global Leadership Development Expert, Executive Coach, Coach Supervisor, Keynote Speaker, Foresight Practitioner, Past Global Chair of International Coaching Federation

As organizations scale, expand through mergers, evolve through changes in leadership and respond to crises, keeping a finger on the pulse of culture becomes more important than ever. Dr. Nooravi shares a fresh lens for looking at culture and defining and redefining it through the company's evolution. When a senior team follows the models in this book, silos, mixed messages and being out of touch with the culture are replaced with an aligned and strategic senior team, cross-functional collaboration, walking the talk and living the company's values. A must-read for every executive.

—**Ashir Hai,** Vice President of IT, Walgreens

Dr. Nooravi has created a playbook for driving an amazing workplace. After years of collaborating with her on our culture, it is great to see her best practices in one place. The conversational tone of her writing mirrors her inspiring personal style of deep listening, coaching and sharing insights. *A Powerful Culture Starts with You* is a must-have book for your company.

—**Donna Vargo,** CEO of Johnson and Jennings General Contracting, 2020 CEO of the Year Finalist by *San Diego Business Journal*, Woman of the Year by *San Diego Magazine*

Dr. Nooravi has shared a formula for success for leaders of any industry who want to drive an engaging and powerful culture from the top. *A Powerful Culture Starts with You* demonstrates how to pay attention to your culture, support a coaching culture and make sure your leaders (in our case administrators, physician leaders and patient advocates) are on the same page, driving the same vision. I highly recommend this book for all leaders who want to achieve strong sustainable results through engaged and motivated teams.

—**Pablo Velez,** CEO, Sharp Chula Vista Medical Center

An evolutionary leadership book that guides the reader toward holistic thinking and authentic being. The book is reader-friendly and full of illustrative stories of metamorphosis. A real treasure for aspiring leaders looking to advance the art and science of working with others to create a world that works for all of us.

—**Jan Phillips,** author of
The Art of Original Thinking: The Making of a Thought Leader

Dr. Nooravi is a highly sought-after speaker and coach who has the experience to answer the question on many business leaders' minds—how do I retain my employees and attract top talent to my company in these difficult times? The answers are in this well-researched book. The right book from the right author at the right time. If you can read only one book this year, I recommend that it be this one.

—**David B. Kinnear,** CEO of dbkAssociates, Vistage Chair,
Board Certified Coach, Certified Veteran Development Coach

Dr. Nooravi's book addresses the heart and soul of what enables an organization to thrive—its people and culture. This body of work is the codification of Dr. Nooravi's depth of experience listening to and coaching executives from a broad range of industries who serve a diverse employee and customer base. I am inspired by how she has crystallized her observations and learnings into an intuitive "how to" for engaged leaders around the world.

—**Dave Feldman,** Chief Operating Officer, Progress Residential

In her book, *A Powerful Culture Starts with You*, Dr. Nooravi discusses the most critical aspect of long-term enterprise success: creating and sustaining a positive work culture. Her book provides a comprehensive framework on which leaders can build their unique company cultures. I have had the opportunity to see Dr. Nooravi in action. She lives what she teaches, and her proven success, illustrated in the case studies she discusses, shows how the principles she conveys can be used as the basis for any company's successful culture road map.

—**Prentice Tom,** MD, Chief Medical Officer at Kintsugi
and Futurist at Vituity

In this book, Dr. Nooravi addresses one of the most important determinants of a successful organization, its culture. She does so from the very grounded basis of direct experience with many individual clients and teams over a period of years. I have worked with Dr. Nooravi, and I know her to be rigorous in her observations and analysis and committed to practical solutions that work. Read it if you are willing to get to work on yourself and your leadership.

—**Dwight Frindt,** Co-Founder 2130 Partners, Vistage Master Chair
& Best Practice Chair, Winner of the prestigious Don Cope Memorial
Award, Investor Activist in the Global Hunger Project for 46 years

A Powerful Culture Starts with You is the ultimate road map to cultural transformation for leaders in any industry. Dr. Nooravi has found a way to seamlessly marry her deep knowledge of organizational dynamics with her "we're going deep" coaching style. The result is a highly accessible and practical framework for culture change, complete with tools and action steps to guide you through the critical reflection and coaching necessary to shape a powerful organizational culture from the inside out.

—**Robin Keith,** CEO, EcoLeaders

This book covers the concepts of culture, leadership and performance on both a personal and corporate level. I highly recommend this timely book and have enjoyed being introduced to the author's concepts, knowledge, and the new look into the relationship between the corporate culture and the end goal of businesses and nonprofits.

—**Mariam Khosravani,** Founder Iranian American
Women Foundation (IAWF)

We are in an incredibly challenging time with regard to hiring and retention. Creating, fostering, and maintaining a strong and flourishing corporate culture has never been more important. Dr. Nooravi has provided the necessary playbook for implementing and maintaining a thriving culture in an organization. I have known Dr. Nooravi for more than a decade and she most definitely can "Walk the Talk."

—**John Van Deusen,** Founder FRS Executive Search

A Powerful Culture Starts with You reveals a unique, three-step prescription for ailing organizational cultures, showcased by compelling true client stories that illuminate the masterful coaching strategies of the author. Dr. Nooravi draws from a deep well of expertise, experience and care. In this book, she shares her secrets of creating a powerful culture with the world.

—**Sandra Younger,** author, speaker, coach,
Founder and Principal, Terra Nova Coaching and Consulting

Many books on organizational culture exist, but none provide a practical and business-minded solution to addressing issues that cause leaders to get stuck as this one does. Dr. Nooravi will take you through a disciplined process that will require you to do some soul searching and develop a comprehensive plan to establish a sustainable and positive work environment that will improve you and your team's performance. The investment you make by reading this book will deliver huge returns!

—**Dave Oates,** CEO, APR, PR Security Service,
author, speaker, trainer

In *A Powerful Culture Starts with You*, Dr. Nooravi gives readers and listeners a peek into the world of executive coaching, sharing coaching conversations and how she empowers leaders to tap into their agency, voice and power. My favorite part of this book is the DRIVE IT model in which she shares tools for driving a coaching conversation, from discovering the challenge, to dreaming of how the leader wants things to be, to getting out of their comfort zone, to taking a small step toward change.

—**Nancy Tylim,** Executive Coach, Mentor coach,
Master Certified Coach (MCC)

Developing diverse and inclusive work spaces is no longer a novelty, but a mandate. Dr. Nooravi gets this and does a masterful job of bringing the reader along for the journey. The models she outlines are both accessible and easy to remember for the busy executive.

—**Dana Smith,** Principal, Exalt Resources

As companies across the United States cope with the Great Resignation, Dr. Nooravi's book is more important and relevant than ever. I particularly like the first-person voice and the personalized approach to her writing. It feels like the author is speaking directly to the reader. This book is a must-read for corporate and entrepreneurial leaders who want to attract and retain the best employees in their industry.

—**Dr. Lori Baker-Schena,** professional speaker and leadership coach

Dr. Shahrzad Nooravi reminds us to look within and keep ourselves accountable to the culture we are trying to create and maintain, offering practical tools and real-life examples to guide us through.

—**Mojgan Momenan,** Associate, AIA, Director,
Danielian Associates Architects + Planners,
Orange County Business Journal, Best Places to Work, 2021

A Powerful Culture Starts with You is a unique and significant contribution to the field of organizational development. Dr. Nooravi draws on her many years of hands-on experience in the field, breaking down culture in three simple steps and offering guidance in applying these concepts.

—**Toni Knott,** PhD, Alliant International University

The culture of an organization is at the core of everything. I have learned so much from Dr. Nooravi's book—to always start from myself, my own fears, expectations, limitations and strengths, and not to be afraid of change.

—**Elena Epstein,** MBA, Creative Director and
Co-owner of *L.A. Parent* magazine

Dr. Nooravi's book gives many tools for how we can regularly pay attention to our culture and how we can coach our staff to drive a patient-centric culture. I recommend this book for all healthcare leaders who want to both engage their physicians and healthcare staff while driving patient care.

—**Andres Smith,** Medical Director of Sharp Chula Vista Medical Center, Department of Emergency Medical Services, Chairman of the Board, Mexican Red Cross, Tijuana, BC

Hallelujah! It's about time somebody with Dr. Nooravi's experience and expertise explained the "how" of improving culture. I highly recommend this book if you would like to demystify the biggest leverage point for business success: culture!

—**Michele Jewett,** advisor & coach, Q4 Leaders

The templates and stories provided in *A Powerful Culture Starts with You* take the guesswork out of cultivating a winning culture and provide powerful, actionable and relatable guidance. I was captivated and educated by the strength of the content and the ease of application contained in this must-read business book.

—**Melissa Priest,** Founder & CEO, Alexandretta Transportation Consulting, Inc., author, entrepreneur, business leader, speaker

As our clients wade through unforeseen challenges with retention, Dr. Nooravi's insights are invaluable. I highly recommend this book as a go-to resource for battling the new talent war.

—**Hollie Packman,** CEO, Packman & Associates, Inc.

At the time of the Great Resignation, creating a strong workplace is more important than ever. This inspiring how-to guide shows how change is possible—when you start from within!

—**Scott Krawitz,** CEO, SAK Consulting

DEDICATION

I am humbled by seeing transformational leadership growth among my clients on a regular basis. This book is dedicated to my past, present and future clients and to all leaders who are ready to do the inner work that makes possible the outer results of strong leadership and a powerful culture. Serving you is a joy and a privilege.

A big thank you to my amazing family, colleagues and friends.

Momma Bear, thank you for making the world a better place with your presence and for always supporting my dreams; telling me not only to go for it but also asking, "What are you waiting for?"

Thank you to my father, who is here with us in spirit. In my weakest moments, he would keep me focused on difficult goals by saying, "Don't give up, don't give up, don't give up!"

To my husband Karrar: Thank you for your joyful spirit and your go-for-it attitude in life and everything I seek to pursue.

CONTENTS

TABLES

PREFACE

Your past is not your potential.
In any hour you can choose to liberate the future.
—Marilyn Ferguson

What Keeps You up at Night versus the Dream

"I'm not sure what's going on with my company," the owner of a manufacturing company emailed me. "There's a heavy feeling of bad vibes, and people seem to be doing just enough to get by. What can I do about these clock-watchers?"

A VP at a professional services firm said, "I'm tired. I'm giving this company my all, and it's never enough. I'm making things work at home with my husband and daughter, but I don't feel settled or like I'm thriving in any particular area—I'm just getting by. Something has to give."

"I create goals with our senior team. The eight of us agree, but then I hear that they're giving different directions to our team members and just doing whatever the hell they want. How can I get everyone on the same page?" asked the director of a global retail organization.

"Our company has been successful despite operating virtually for almost two years now," a CEO told me in a conference call. "I still look forward to staff coming back into the office in some capacity, even though I know employees across the country are rejecting it. I'm not sure how to manage this."

Do you ever stay up at night wondering about these types of challenges? The behaviors, decisions and attitudes you see throughout your company, or maybe from yourself, somehow don't meet your expectations for how things should be.

I know that you, as an entrepreneur, founder, director, or leader, are working hard to make your company profitable. There can be pressure coming from your board, employees and customers. You may hear that your company needs to make products more quickly, but you worry about quality and mistakes. Your staff may tell you that the company needs to create more methodologies, yet there never seems to be enough time to slow down and do it, because your company moves on to the next thing quickly. Balancing growth and structure is hard!

You may dream of a workplace where employees arrive smiling, in a good mood, with a positive attitude and the willingness to do whatever it takes to get the job done—to make the company highly profitable with top-quality products and services and happy clients who want more. It's a great dream—one you probably imagine in short bursts during times of stress before sighing out loud and dismissing it. "How am I supposed to make these people better? Where do I even start?"

Tapping into Your Personal Power

All outer change begins with inner work. Our personal power is revealed when we create space. When we put our frustrations on pause and take a deep breath; when we release our assumptions, triggers, fears, egos, history, storylines and ideas of how things should be; when we practice being open, curious and self-realizing, we can create the change we dream of.

Many leaders get stuck by approaching external problems with external solutions when our true power lies within. Being open to the work of discovering our deepest potential is not only transformative but also propels us along the path of going deeper and achieving more. Yes, it will bring you material success, but more than that, a sense of presence, calm and confidence that empowers you to be the change you want to see everywhere you go.

When you own your power, you have agency, and you will realize that every powerful transformation begins by looking within and tapping into your personal power. This is what forms the root of culture.

Who I Am and What I Know

I am an organizational psychologist and Master Certified Coach (MCC, as certified by the International Coaching Federation), and I have worked with leaders of mid-sized to Fortune 500 companies over the last two decades. I work with bright leaders who want more for their lives and their company cultures. They want stronger team dynamics and increased engagement, excitement and energy for their staff. They also dream of being more innovative and self-expressed and having more balance. By collaborating with these clients—including through asking meaningful questions and gently challenging their views—I've supported them to manage change, inspire employees and drive productivity.

Creating a strong culture is possible. I've seen it over and over again. The thousands of conversations I've had with clients have helped me to see the beauty in human potential. My clients have marveled at how, after they changed their actions and mindsets, people around them started shifting and growing, too. When smart leaders are motivated and possess the right tools and support, the impossible becomes possible.

In *A Powerful Culture Starts with You: Cultivate a Thriving Workplace from the Inside Out*, I will share with you my experience in applying the principles of organization theory, change management, behavioral psychology, personality and motivation coupled with the knowledge I have gained by partnering with and empowering leaders to tap into new capabilities, mindsets and behaviors. With an investment of your time, an openness to seeing your part, and a determination to take consistent action, you can realize your vision of being a powerful leader of an amazing team, company and culture. The dream doesn't have to stay a dream. I will show you how to make your vision a reality.

The thousands of conversations I've had with clients have helped me to see the beauty in human potential. My clients marvel at how changing their actions and mindsets has helped people around them to start shifting and growing, too.

My Inspiration for Writing This Book

I wrote *A Powerful Culture Starts with You* after two decades of working with companies as an internal consultant and running my own practice for a decade. I was bursting to share my knowledge on methods and processes that have empowered leaders to tap into their wisdom, power, resilience and grace. These are four core elements that expand and improve life holistically. Three experiences served as the impetus for writing this book:

The first encompasses the many coaching conversations I have had with smart, talented leaders. I have the privilege of coaching and empowering leaders to tap into their deepest talents, get out of their comfort zone, and push on despite imposter syndrome and their egos and fears. It is a gift to observe leaders transform and become more confident, emotionally intelligent and comfortable in their own skin despite constant change, conflict, or frustrations. In this book, I share the patterns I've seen and how I've partnered with leaders to be the change they would like to see.

The second was the plea I frequently heard from C-level executives, directors and managers: "Culture is ambiguous. Please tell me what to do." This book is designed to do just that using three models I created expressly for this purpose: WATCH IT guides readers to find new ways of observing their culture and recognizing common Culture Stressors. DRIVE IT® supports readers to examine their own thinking. WALK IT® focuses on skills needed to sustain a strong culture from the top. Once you take on and drive one change successfully using these models, you will know how to drive other changes.

The third is the knowledge that when leaders invest in their own leadership through coaching for themselves and their teams, whole companies can transform; disengaged or minimally engaged employees can develop an ownership mindset, treating the company as if it's their own. Nothing delights me more than employees who say, "What have you done with my boss? She's working with us in a way that's motivating and inspiring, and our environment reflects this change."

Employee engagement is especially important as the landscape of work evolves. Work environments have been and will be impacted by the COVID-19 pandemic, with more work happening virtually and global connectivity increasing. The need for supporting diversity, equity and inclusion in the workplace remains strong and has come more clearly into focus for many. We are navigating new ways of working that balance the technology that enables virtual work with the relationship-building that happens through in-person and virtual interactions.

A Powerful Culture Starts with You is designed for current and future C-suite executives, corporate officers, entrepreneurs, HR leaders, managers and individuals who care about company culture and growth. These are the people who have input into shaping and reshaping culture; with their advocacy, they can drive cultures that are open, inclusive, powerful and engaging. Improving your culture builds pride among employees, enhances the customer experience, and makes your company a desirable place to work. These types of cultures support longer-term retention of high-performing staff and strengthen the company's reputation.

Our Evolving Landscape

I've tried to make *A Powerful Culture Starts with You* as evergreen as possible, given our quickly evolving environment amidst a global pandemic. Changes in how we work together virtually; technology that can empower and halt communication; the expanded focus on diversity, equity and inclusion in all that we do; and generations in the workplace are a few of the areas that will continue to be factors in our organizational planning and thinking.

The global COVID-19 pandemic has brought anguish for many individuals and families as they faced illness and the unexpected untimely deaths of their loved ones. There has been controversy about the timing of opening and closing schools and businesses. Everyone has been affected, whether through grief and loss; health concerns; companies closing; job loss; parents having to work from home and support virtual learning; children being away from their classmates and friends; teachers multitasking and doing their best operating in a completely different format; rising rates of mental health conditions and domestic violence; and living with the unknown, month after month.

Many people have also found positives in the ease of connecting globally and finding new ways to work remotely. Commutes were reduced; families spent more time together (including showing up in the background of our video calls); and we found that work does continue. We didn't fall apart. We adapted to working virtually. According to a PulseSecure report[1] the majority (84 percent) of US organizations expect a broader and more permanent remote work adoption after the coronavirus pandemic eases. Many companies already have decided to switch to long-term remote work[2] including Adobe, Amazon, Capital One, Dropbox, Facebook, Ford Motor Company, Microsoft, Salesforce, Target and Verizon.

. . . .

1. Cybersecurity Insiders, "Remote Work from Home Cybersecurity Report," PulseSecure, 2020, https://rs.ivanti.com/reports/ivi-2537-wfh-cyber-security-report.pdf?psredirect.
2. FlexJobs, "Companies Switching to Long-Term Remote Work," FlexJobs, accessed on August 14, 2021, https://www.flexjobs.com/blog/post/companies-switching-remote-work-long-term.

Whether we go back to being in the office full time, or create better options for working virtually, or some hybrid, ensuring the cohesion of teams and energy and drive of individuals will be key. Some people love working virtually and resist going back to the way things were while some want the old normal. What work schedules will be right for your company? How will you work with the generations in your workplace? How can you support diversity, equity and inclusion in your workplace? How will you develop ways to educate your employees on what bias is and how it shows up? How will you create a workplace that is inclusive, where people feel welcomed to share who they are?

The section on Culture Cultivators offers ideas for how to infuse remote work with connection as you design your culture. It also covers how diversity and inclusion contribute to innovation and a happier workforce, and how to involve and respect the generations in the workplace.

Empowered and Ready

From the C-suite, to managers, to production staff, to new employees, tending to a company's culture is everyone's responsibility. The best-case scenario is that you develop and empower all your employees to be Culture Guardians: people who believe in the company, do everything they can to alert others when something is going wrong, and take time to contribute to the fix. Every leader should listen to what employees talk about, pay attention to team dynamics and notice when things are going wrong. The human resources manager can be both the problem-solver who employees feel safe going to and the strategic partner who proposes and drives needed changes. By empowering your team to share their voices, you share power and give a voice to those who can drive the changes you want to see.

Once you begin viewing yourself and your culture through the lens shared in *A Powerful Culture Starts with You*, there will be no going back. You will confirm what you know, realize answers to ongoing nagging problems, and gain a deeper understanding of concepts you may have had some idea about but couldn't quite articulate. Negative self-talk or imposter syndrome feelings will be transformed into agency, confidence and standing tall—standing up for yourself. You will feel empowered and ready to be the change you want to see.

Time and again, I've seen this happen firsthand for my clients. The manufacturing firm owner who emailed me was able to grow his team from disengaged to engaged; from worrying about when they were leaving to being committed to results; from bad vibes and quietness to positive energy and joy. The VP of the professional services firm reviewed her tasks and meetings, negotiated, and cleared time for the most strategic work. She enjoys taking her daughter to her martial arts classes twice a week and making time for self-care. The director of the global retail organization got his team on the same page, supporting one another and having the courage to speak up when they disagreed. They comfortably call each other out when a decision may not be aligned with the company values. It's no surprise that he's in a good mood. The CEO whose first instinct was to have everyone return to the office is working with a task force of employees to create a hybrid approach that supports employees' desire to work remotely and the CEO's desire for an in-person workplace that supports human connection.

I welcome you to this journey of self-discovery, self-empowerment, and tapping into your best, most powerful self for expanded holistic success professionally and personally.

It's in Your Hands!

Your time
+
Your openness and curiosity
+
Determination and grit

Realizing your vision for an amazing culture

PART 1
THE FOUNDATION OF CULTURE

Culture Is a Living Organism

I am intrigued by the beauty of trees and the ways in which they make a vital difference in our lives—from providing oxygen, shade, beauty, flowers and fruits to greenery and a sense of community. What we see is the tree itself in all its splendor. What we don't see are the deep roots that serve as the source of the tree's power and strength. If a tree is taken care of from the roots, it will thrive on the outside. What you nourish is what will thrive and grow.

A company's culture is also a living organism that needs nourishing and care. When a company is healthy, it provides stability, revenue and products; services that make a difference to consumers; good wages to employees; and a chance for people to tap into their potential and grow with the company. The company can provide a place for employees to feel safe, be productive and experience joy. These are the results you can see.

Your company is rooted in the behaviors, viewpoints and decisions that reflect the seeds planted by the founders and leaders of the company. Nourishing these roots—the values, behaviors and decisions; its leadership and staff—supports the company and its ability to thrive. Your people hold down the company, cultivate it and make sure it thrives. To be successful, a company must continually work on nourishing these elements underneath the surface so that deep-rooted behaviors are healthy and can withstand time, changing conditions and storms. The stronger the roots, the more the company can be resilient during crises and difficult times, whether changes in industry, technology, competition, or worldwide challenges such as pandemics.

The roots of your culture are formed by factors such as your assumptions, views about work, cultural upbringing, views about gender roles, political views, the generation in which you grew up, your ethnic background, how you learned to respond to conflict growing up, your biases and personality type. If you ever want to change something in your culture, you may need to examine your assumptions about employees and the environment.

I wrote *A Powerful Culture Starts with You* because I know you can drive the change you want to see by being the change you want to see. When you think about culture as a living thing, you can think about your relationship to it and what's necessary to keep this relationship alive and healthy. Similar to having a relationship with someone you care about, you don't just do one nice thing and stop. You invest time, attention, and care consistently. Culture is a living organism that you must keep alive and thriving by investing in it and caring for it continuously.

A Powerful Culture Starts with You will empower you to examine how you are tending to your company—your tree. You will look at what behaviors and leadership styles are strengthening your tree (Culture Cultivators) and which ones are weakening your tree (Culture Stressors). You will have a chance to consider how well you and your Culture Guardians are examining (WATCH IT) your tree, coming up with new leadership behaviors (DRIVE IT), and sustaining the tree's care (WALK IT).

What Is Culture?

Before we dive in, let's make sure we're on the same page about organizational culture and what shapes it. On this journey, it may help to also think of company culture as the personality of your company—a personality that is expressed through the behaviors of your leaders. If you think about your own personality, you know that you have your strengths and areas where you shine and some areas that can use some work. (Like when you lose your s——t when your people mess something up, even though you're working on taking a more Zen approach to life.) Just as you have beliefs, attitudes, habits and assumptions drawn from your life experiences that inform how you do things, so does your company. Just as you make decisions in a certain way, so does your company. Why? Because these ways of being have been transmitted from you, the company founders and leaders, into the fabric of the workplace environment, bit by bit, over time.

Over three decades ago, organization development theorist Edgar Schein found that there are five ways culture is shared and creates values, beliefs and attitudes: (1) what we pay attention to; (2) how we react in crises; (3) what is role-modeled; (4) how we allocate rewards; and (5) how we bring people on and dismiss them.[3] These all hold true today. I add to this list a sixth factor: what is important to your people and to the current generation in general and how leaders respond to this.

Culture is not some vague thing, out there. It's a collection of behaviors by a group of people. Each leader has ways of responding to people, projects and challenges. It's about what is rewarded (individual, group, and/or collective performance). It's what people appreciate and what they complain about. It's how customers are treated. It's how department leaders work together. It's how we lead, how we respond and how we react.—All of these behaviors combined make up the personality of the organization—the company culture. Culture is the mind, heart and soul of an organization.

These behaviors and the assumptions, beliefs and experiences they are based on can be seen as the root of culture. As you take the steps to examine your workplace, you are examining the health of the trunk, you are looking at the leaf strength and quality. You are also looking at the soil to see if the tree is hydrated and nourished. There may be Culture Cultivators that make this tree thrive and Culture Stressors that hurt it. On this journey, the more Culture Guardians you educate and engage to assist you, the better the health of your company will be.

Working on Culture Improves Your Company and Bottom Line

Okay, you've gotten this far. The topic of culture is resonating with you. Now you might be wondering, "How does culture impact my company's profitability?" Great question and the right question. Why go through the time and effort of investing in your culture if you don't know what the outcomes will be?

First, a negative culture impacts your bottom line. Consequences include reduced productivity through absenteeism, turnover, and losing your most talented people; the cost of training new people and the impact on sales until you get them up to speed; the damage to your company's reputation; and lackluster performance, to name a few.

....

3.   Edgar Schein, *Organizational Culture and Leadership,* 5th ed. (Jossey-Bass Business Series, 2016).

WISDOM
POWER
RESILIENCE
GRACE

POSITIVE COURAGE MINDFULNESS   OPTIMISM COMMUNITY BOLD
SUSTAINABLE VISUALIZE AUTHENTICITY CHANGE AGENT VISION INTENTION
LEADER AS COACH WALK THE TALK CO-CREATE & INNOVATE
VALUES PURPOSE INCLUSIVE CUSTOMERS FIRST

Companies that invest in their culture are more profitable over time as they attract quality candidates and save time and money on recruiting.[4] Gallup research shows that companies with above-average levels of employee engagement enjoy 147 percent higher earnings per share.[5] Other ways that companies benefit financially from creating a strong culture are less absenteeism, less turnover, less management required, higher morale and healthier employees.[6]

However, there are also many profitable companies that do not invest in their culture as much as they perhaps should. Companies like K-Mart, Forever 21, Wal-Mart and Ross had booming years—until they didn't. K-Mart and Forever 21 have closed the majority of their stores. Wal-Mart continues to be

4. Glassdoor Team, "Why Investing in Your Culture Is Worth It," Glassdoor for Employers (blog) Glassdoor, May 28, 2015, https://www.glassdoor.com/employers/blog/why-investing-in-your-culture-is-worth-it.

5. Susan Sorenson, "How Employee Engagement Drives Growth," Gallup, June 20, 2013, https://www.gallup.com/workplace/236927/employee-engagement-drives-growth.aspx.

6. William Craig, "8 Ways Your Company Culture Directly Impacts Your Bottom Line," Forbes, November 21, 2017, https://www.forbes.com/sites/williamcraig/2017/11/21/8-ways-your-company-culture-directly-impacts-your-bottom-line.

profitable but at the price of constant churn. Some companies are okay with constant turnover and "getting on that damn list again," as long as they are profitable. More recent examples of worst-rated companies to work for are Office Max, Family Dollar, Dollar General, GameStop, Steak 'n Shake and Williams-Sonoma[7] for a combination of reasons ranging from low wages and toxic culture to high turnover.

Glassdoor is a US-based website where employees can review companies anonymously.[8] Each year, Glassdoor publishes a list of lowest-ranked places to work based on the number of current and former employees who take the time to write about their experience at the company. "Yeah, yeah," leaders say, "only the disgruntled go there." True—*and* when there is a trend of several thousand workers talking about poor working conditions, minimum wage and a lack of attention to workers' well-being at the same company, you have a culture that does not value people.

The crux of the issue here is people and profits. We're talking about the long-term success that comes from people who are invested in and loyal to your company and how to grow that type of company culture. If that's what you want, keep reading.

Awesome Company Cultures Are Awesome by Design
Let's talk about what it looks and feels like when leaders tend to their culture and people. Think about your own experience as a consumer. I often ask leaders in my workshops to describe their favorite stores and what makes them special. Where do they feel happy and satisfied as a shopper? What's their experience when culture is done right?

Over the years, hundreds of leaders have shared a similar list of the top twenty stores they, as consumers, admire for the service and culture. Companies that have positive consumer reputations include Container Store, In-N-Out Burger and Starbucks, to name a few. People describe the cultures at these stores as inviting and comfortable. They say employees go out of their way to serve their needs. My clients go back to these places repeatedly and tell others about them, too.

. . . .

7.   Serah Louis, "Worker Beware: These Are the 22 Worst Companies to Work For," MoneyWise, December 10, 2020, https://moneywise.com/managing-money/employment/the-worst-companies-to-work-for.

8.   Glassdoor, https://www.glassdoor.com.

A positive workplace culture is critical to millennials, who will comprise 75 percent of the work population by 2025.[9] A great culture makes your company more profitable and attractive to potential employees. People spend most of their time at work and want it to be a growth-oriented, joyful place.

People use words like warm, clean, friendly and fresh when they talk about Whole Foods. From the physical environment and the way things are spaced out well; to the clean, warm wood floors, high ceilings and organized aisles; to the staff who respond to your needs, you feel welcome and confident about finding what you need. At Nordstrom, racks are set up at a distance that's comfortable for walking around, and sales team members are knowledgeable and friendly.

At Costco, there is another kind of culture: friendly and efficient, fast-paced. They make returns simple. They also pick the best products for their customers. Back in the day, my father used to come home with various handheld electronic devices (think Palm Pilots in the early 2000s or digital cameras—what are those?). When I would ask him why he'd bought the item, he'd always respond with, "That's what Costco had!" And we'd have a laugh, because I understood. He trusted the company and the people who chose the products.

At Apple stores, what you may first notice is the clean, white open space. There are people buzzing about learning, problem-solving, and trying out the newest version of an iThing. Have you noticed that Apple employees look like you and me? You'll find the young hip employee with cool blue hair working next to a Filipina lady in her forties, alongside a differently abled gentleman in a wheelchair, by an African American senior citizen colleague. This is by design. Having such diversity ensures that customers can relate to Apple store employees.

These companies are not awesome by accident. They work at their culture from beginning to end. They are clear about who they want on their team, how they train people, the work environment and the management that they provide. And, of course, they are fair with wages and benefits. However, believe it or not, according to recent research, "56% of workers ranked a

9. Danny Becket Jr. "The Millennial Takeover: How the Generation Is Shaking up the Workplace," *Entrepreneur*, July 21, 2020, https://www.entrepreneur.com/article/353284.

strong workplace culture as more important than salary"[10] Most people will accept less pay, being willing to give up "23% of their entire future lifetime earnings in order to have a job that was always meaningful."[11] Why would that be? Because we live at our companies and spend more time there than with our families. Does that mean creating a great culture is a shortcut to lower wages? Not if you wish to provide competitive and comfortable living wages that will keep your high performers longer and empower people to support their families.

From Toxic to Healthy

Awesome cultures are joyful and energizing for the employees and customers. Toxic cultures have driven 20 percent of US employees out of their jobs in the past five years, at a turnover cost greater than $223 billion.[12] Six of ten people reported leaving their workplace because of their managers, and three in ten because their manager did not encourage a culture of open and transparent communication.[13] Sadly, one in four say they dread going to work, don't feel safe voicing their opinions, and don't feel respected.[14]

Leadership training and coaching will help create kinder, more effective leaders who drive performance and accountability in motivating ways. The senior team plays a crucial role in communicating and role-modeling the leadership they desire from their reports and redirecting behaviors that stray from this standard and violate company values.

. . . .

10. Chloe Taylor, "Workers Value a Strong Company Culture over Higher Pay, Study Claims," CNBC Make It, July 11, 2019, https://www.cnbc.com/2019/07/11/workers-value-a-strong-company-culture-over-higher-pay-study-claims.html.

11. Shawn Achor and others, "9 out of 10 People Are Willing to Earn Less Money to Do More-Meaningful Work," *Harvard Business Review,* November 6, 2018, https://hbr.org/2018/11/9-out-of-10-people-are-willing-to-earn-less-money-to-do-more-meaningful-work.

12. SHRM, "SHRM Reports Toxic Workplace Cultures Cost Billions," SHRM, September 25, 2019, https://www.shrm.org/about-shrm/press-room/press-releases/Pages/SHRM-Reports-Toxic-Workplace-Cultures-Cost-Billions.aspx.

13. SHRM, Toxic Workplaces.

14. Ibid.

Following are examples of behaviors that can contribute to a toxic culture:

- Saying one thing and doing another, or not walking the talk.
- Leaving employees unprotected from an inappropriate work environment. This includes how you manage inappropriate and abusive behavior in the workplace, from sexual harassment to emotional abuse, and creating a culture that supports reporting unethical behavior in the workplace without fear of consequences.
- Excusing poor behavior because the leader is a high performer.
- Having a leadership team that is not diverse or that does not value diversity.
- Not promoting or giving voice to women in the organization; not calling out exclusive behavior that promotes a boys' club culture and excludes women and minorities.
- Having an uncomfortable workplace that does not value employee welfare.

Throughout my career, I have noted that there are some specific patterns that smart, well-intentioned leaders can fall into that end up damaging culture. I call these Culture Stressors. Culture Stressors contribute to a difficult workplace where leaders feel unsure of where to focus their energies or disconnected, unable to perform their best work; and staff feel unmotivated or not heard. You can read more in this book about Culture Stressors as well as their antidote: Culture Cultivators. These are best practices for creating a thriving, powerful, resilient culture that calls out and counteracts the problems that can lead to a toxic workplace.

Culture Guardians

You may be thinking, "Things are all right in my company. We're profitable. Good people are staying. When I ask for feedback, everyone says, 'Things are fine.' What's the relevance here for me?" The hard work you've dedicated to building your culture must be maintained. Is everything really "fine"? Is "fine" where you want things to be?

If you've recently had a leadership retreat off-site, shared the strategy with all employees, sought engagement feedback and had team-building events—awesome. Those are all great things. How do you know the impact of these actions on your employees? The answer is Culture Guardians.

A Culture Guardian is a committed employee who treats the company as if it were their own. They may be employed throughout different levels of the company, but they are all concerned about the company's health and well-being financially and culturally. Some employees are intrinsically driven and will keep you apprised of the state of the culture's health, while others can be trained and encouraged to do so. Culture Guardians are change agents who should be empowered.

I'm sure you can think of a handful of people like this, especially if you've been empowering them. These are not spies who skulk around seeking gossip about others. Culture Guardians are team members who care deeply. It's the person who will tell you after an all-hands meeting, "A lot of people didn't really understand the strategy you shared and felt it was complicated. Maybe you need to distill the information." It's the employee who emails to let you know, "Three people told me Jim was yelling at staff. This has to stop."

You can encourage Culture Guardians by thanking these brave souls for taking the risk to give you feedback. You can act where you believe it is warranted. You can be vulnerable and ask for honest feedback. Educating, engaging with and empowering Culture Guardians is a way to tap more deeply into your employees' potential. Once your Culture Guardians are clear on the values and the type of culture you want to drive, tell them what you are looking for. For example: What are people excited about? What suggestions do they have? Is there anything that is distressing staff? What ideas do they have for improvements?

Who Do You Want to Be?
There is no one-size-fits-all culture. You can design the culture you want to create. Your ability to improve your culture and grow your team depends on your becoming clear about who you want to be and what culture you want to design. Since a big part of culture stems from the leader and the leader's efforts and inner work, determining your values is a first step. Consider identifying five values you'd like to live by. Ask yourself how you can live these values for yourself, your team, your family and your community.

Managing Your Time
Your values may include connections (positive work and family relationships), well-being (health, fitness and personal time), and professional excellence. Living to these values requires time and attention, two things that often elude us. *Wow, it's 5:00 p.m.? Thursday? Um, it's March already?* Time is elusive, precious, and quickly escapes us if we do not protect it. Year after year, clients tell me about the challenges they face with a lack of work-life balance.

They take dinner breaks and then log back on for a few more hours of work and rarely feel like they can unplug and become present and relaxed. Clients have shared that they "feel like I'm tethered to my phone, on call at all hours."

Clients also say that they have so many meetings that they hardly have time to perform the deep thinking and strategic work they are skilled to do and paid for. "I barely have time between meetings for a restroom break, let alone to write down my actions and email others about theirs. The only time I get any quiet for long-term strategizing and visioning the future is after 5:00 p.m. It's getting exhausting, and I'm burning out," a VP told me when we started leadership coaching.

This section outlines ways to create time (and protect it!) so that you spend your effort on what's most strategic for your organization. The following techniques have helped hundreds of clients gain their time back. No, not so that you can come up with more work to do, but so that you can work strategically and carve out time for family, recharging, and experiences that bring joy.

Task Analysis

A task review involves listing all the main tasks you are responsible for (Table 1). Add the purpose of the task, how long it takes, how strategic it is on a scale of 1-10, and who else can help support this task. Once you have captured your main tasks, take a step back and review them. How many tasks are not strategic in nature and taking up your time? Who can help you with them? What's that—it will take too much time to train the person? Yes, in the short term, it may take a few sessions to ensure the person taking on the task learns how to do it. It will also take managing your expectations and getting okay with the fact that it may not be done your way. In the long term, though, it gets the task off your plate, helps someone else grow, and gives you more time to work on what is most important.

TABLE 1. Task Analysis Form

Task	Purpose	Time required	Strategic 1-10	Support for task

Meeting Analysis

A meeting review is similar in that it helps you determine which meetings most warrant receiving your attention and efforts, which are important for team building, which are occasional FYIs, and which should be delegated, shortened, etc. (Table 2). Create and protect your time so that your efforts are spent on the areas that are most strategic for your organization. You can do this by delegating, opting out, negotiating, shortening and keeping what is most important for your schedule.

TABLE 2. Meeting Analysis Form

Meeting	Purpose	Time required	Strategic 1-10	Options: Delegate / Opt out / Negotiate how often to attend / Shorten / Keep

Many of my clients who complete the task and meeting analyses find five to ten hours a week, if not more, that they can reallocate. They become protective of their time and block off hours for thinking time and encourage their staff to do the same. They report designing and delivering more ideas, which leads to innovation. They also start protecting scheduled blocks to eat, exercise and relax. Most report feeling more refreshed and recharged. Some clients share that eating dinner with their family has become the norm rather than an exception. One key is to create and protect these times with boundaries for starting and stopping. Granted, this may not be applicable to times when there's a big project that will require extra time or when the team needs all hands on deck. This is about your week-to-week, month-to-month life balance.

The Esteem Portfolio

When it comes to work-life balance, an esteem portfolio may empower you to expand the areas where you recharge and gain esteem outside of work. Self-esteem is an individual's subjective evaluation of their own worth. It encompasses beliefs about the self as well as the emotional states we experience, such as pride and joy in our successes and despair and shame in our disappointments and perceived failures. Along your path, as you pay attention to expanding your company or department, maximizing revenue, and hopefully ensuring that you are bringing your people along with you, there is one more thing you must care for: you.

Work cannot and should not be the only source from which you gain your esteem. Or, put another way, the only space where you experience positive results and feedback and feel good about yourself. Sure, it is amazing when we make a big difference at work and receive accolades from colleagues and clients. And it may feel good to a degree to put all your energy into work after hours and on weekends as you complete big projects. But what is the impact?

There are many leaders whose children are busy with sports and homework, or who are grown up and out of the house. These leaders think, "I have plenty of space to work, and I've taken care of my obligations." This may be true, and there is something beautiful about having launched your children in the world. Or you may have a spouse who travels constantly, leaving you with free time. You don't have to fill this time with work. "But I can be more productive," you may say. I agree—and I encourage you to expand your portfolio of activities beyond work.

What goes into the esteem portfolio? Anything that contributes to your wellness, joy, calm and sense of esteem. Ideally, you diversify your portfolio so that you're reaping benefits from multiple sources into which you're also investing continuously: work; family; your partner; hobbies; healthy movement; learning; friends; and community.

It's important to know that being good at work and gaining fulfillment and positive reinforcement from that environment, combined with the blueprint of our upbringing—for example, having had parents who worked above and beyond or prioritized work ethic—may arouse work-addicted behavior in some people. A sign of work addiction is gaining esteem and even endorphins from working overtime. If a leader has an addiction to work, it impacts the company culture they develop and creates a sense of pressure and expectation that employees must work on that urgent report and send it back by 9:00 p.m. on a weeknight or by Sunday morning. (Of course, there are times outside the norm when there's a crisis or an urgent board meeting, and the occasional weekend of work or late hours are needed.)

"Well, what would I do instead?" Expanding your esteem portfolio is about coming up with activities that recharge you. Explore the things that are interesting for you. It can be as simple as reading a book; playing golf; cooking a new dish or meeting up with a friend for a hike, walk, or coffee. Maybe it's taking a class in a subject you like, be that sports, art, writing, music, language, or history. These are activities that go beyond family time and date time, which also empower you to nurture your relationships.

Whatever it is, the more you plan on ways to grow, learn and expand your mental and physical abilities, the less you will be likely to get drawn into work. "Why not work?" you may ask. "I'm good at it, and I have time." Let me plant this seed: this life is short, and your health, well-being, and taking time to recharge is part of your job as a leader. Take the time to appreciate yourself and to treat yourself to things that make you feel good. You've got work covered. On a regular basis, add things that will enrich and recharge you.

How to Use *A Powerful Culture Starts with You*

Beginner's Mind

Shoshin, meaning *beginner's mind*, is a concept from Zen Buddhism that refers to "having an attitude of openness, eagerness, and lack of preconceptions when studying a subject, even when studying at an advanced level, just as a beginner would."[15] With a beginner's mind, you try to forget everything you know, or think you know, about a subject and to view it fresh with no experience, expertise, or thoughts on the subject. Developing, and coming back to, a beginner's mind is the way to stay anchored throughout this journey.

Working on your culture may require some new ways of thinking. It may require you to be still and observe your culture from a place of nonjudgment. It may require you to see things from a fresh perspective, pushing assumptions to the side and being curious. You may also need to engage in some deep inner work to ask yourself if and how you have contributed to a particular dynamic. This work also requires you to trust that you have within you the answers to resolve any issue, whether in your company or life. It can be a new behavior to dig deep inside your soul, reflect on what you want, and decide that you have the power and agency to achieve it.

Being Present

Deciding that you are in charge and have the personal power to improve any situation can be scary at worst and empowering at best. It's an opportunity to practice being present, remembering that you have control in the here and now. I contrast being present with being wishful—thinking that you have no control or agency. You can use the Being Wishful to Being Present tool (Table 3) throughout reading this book. If you feel stuck or frustrated or want to throw in the towel, think of this tool as an anchor that will bring you back to the here and now.

....

15. Shoshin sur *Encyclopédie technique, historique, biographique et culturelle des arts martiaux*, 2004.

TABLE 3. Being Wishful to Being Present

Being Wishful	Being Present
Living in the past or anxious about the future	In the here and now
I am seeking something out there, and I	**I am present and willing to**
☐ Avoid.	☐ Discover.
☐ Act on impulse.	☐ Reflect.
☐ Put things off. "You only live once."	☐ Do the work.
I'm a victim, and things happen to me outside of my control.	I take accountability for what's happened in my life.
The answers are out there.	The answers are in here.
Examination of others	**Examination of self**
Here's what's wrong with them.	Who am I? Who do I want to be? How do I affect others?
Judgment of self and others	**Acceptance and compassion for self and others**
People don't change.	I can be better, and this is my path.
I'm an old dog; I can't learn new tricks.	People can grow.
Change is too hard.	Change is totally possible.
High ego	**Low ego**
Short-term thinking and avoids intuition.	Long-term thinking and seeks out intuition.
What is left to learn?	I want to keep learning.
Avoids feedback. "I'm fine how I am."	Seeks feedback from others.
Avoids reflection. "I am who I am."	Questions own assumptions and behaviors. "Why do I think like this?"
Finds it too difficult to look into the past.	Gets to the root of fears and worries.
Avoid old hurts at all costs. "I shouldn't open a can of worms."	Willing to face old hurts for the purpose of future growth.

Abundance Mindset

Another perspective to cultivate is an abundance mindset, where you see life through the lens of abundance: there is plenty to go around. You see the limitless potential and possibility in yourself and others. Rather than seeing someone in your industry as a threat, you see the person as a potential ally or colleague. Rather than thinking there is scarcity, you believe that there is enough for everyone. With this mindset, you are more likely to create the life and results you want.

Your Guide to WATCH IT, DRIVE IT®, WALK IT®

In the next parts of this book, I will share with you the common challenges that leaders of fast-growth organizations face and the three-part model I use—WATCH IT, DRIVE IT, WALK IT—when I partner with them over a period of time (usually six to twelve months) to understand their current culture, define the culture they need to meet their strategy, and clarify the values and behaviors that will help them get there. You will see from this three-part model that creating a strong culture is doable. You will become equipped with tools and techniques to manage challenges and build on successes.

Throughout *A Powerful Culture Starts with You*, I include stories from coaching leaders, facilitating senior teams, and working on the entire culture as it grows and evolves. I share real case studies of coaching conversations that lead to big actions by clients. I also share lessons from some of my own personal transformations and successes. You may see yourself in these stories and examples of Culture Cultivators and Culture Stressors. That's okay and healthy to develop awareness of your strengths and where they may have become overplayed into weaknesses. Suggested reflections and action steps at the end of each section give you an opportunity to reflect on what you've learned and on your potential next steps.

Doing the work in this book empowers you to view your life and company from different angles. In WATCH IT, you are taking a step back and viewing your company culture with fresh eyes so you can become aware of Culture Stressors. In DRIVE IT, you are exploring your challenges from the inside out and developing coaching skills that you can use with yourself and others as you work on the ways you want to grow personally as a leader. In WALK IT, you are viewing your teams from a group dynamic perspective and creating a reset that will impact your team and company so you can sustain the culture you've always wanted.

I designed an acronym for each of these three parts of *A Powerful Culture Starts with You* (Table 4). I use acronyms to break up concepts into practical, doable steps.

TABLE 4. WATCH IT, DRIVE IT®, WALK IT®

WATCH IT	DRIVE IT®	WALK IT®
Examine your culture	Understand where you are stuck and make a plan to DRIVE IT®	Get everyone on the same team, moving in the same direction, and WALK IT® to sustain your success
Walk around	**D**etermine the challenge	**W**alk the talk
Ask, seek, explore	**R**eflect on what making this change would mean to you	**A**lign your senior team
Take in feedback		**L**ook at your culture
Clarify and understand		**K**now your plan
Handle your ego	**I**nvite a new way of thinking	
Inspire a new plan	**V**aliantly get out of your comfort zone	**I**ntegrate values
Take charge of growing yourself and your culture	**E**ngage support	**T**rack everything
	Initiate the first step	
	Transform your thinking to prepare for challenges	

PART 2
EXAMINE YOUR COMPANY CULTURE

Observe Your Culture

When I talk to leaders around the country about company culture, they say repeatedly that they want to know how to understand their culture, particularly during times of transition. "I have a sense of our culture and how we do things. I love to create a great environment and I've learned from experimenting what the staff likes. How can I learn more about my culture on my own? Is there a way to go about it?"

Being asked these questions over the years prompted me to create a brief guide for how leaders can investigate their own culture. These steps will guide you in inspiring new plans and taking charge. There are many things you can discover about your company culture if you slow down and put on your investigator, journalist, or researcher hat. Think of this as a culture study.

Companies experience transitions from time to time, whether bringing in new leaders, acquiring companies, rolling out new products or services, or facing national or global challenges like pandemics or civil unrest. These events impact staff, and leaders must be vigilant about communicating regularly, designing structures for communication and work and preventing breakdowns in teamwork. WATCH IT aids in activating your curiosity switch, shifting your openness to high gear and turning on your culture radar.

The WATCH IT Model

The steps of the WATCH IT model serve to help you pay attention to your culture. Doing this in a present, mindful and curious way involves taking a big step back—zooming out and looking at your culture from an objective, big-picture macro level. The more you practice these steps, the more you will start from a place of openness and curiosity versus indignation and stubbornness.

The WATCH IT Model	
Walk around	Make use of four specialized checklists to engage your senses in observing your workplace in new ways.
Ask, seek, explore	Learn how to further engage others in your culture study.
Take in feedback	Gather insights and opinions from your teams with a mix of new and old-school methods.
Clarify and understand	Differentiate between reality, perceptions and blind spots when examining feedback.
Handle your ego	Breathe in others' input without blowing out fire and venom. Use this section as a guide for asking deeper questions and preparing mentally and emotionally to accept different viewpoints in a more open, nonattached way.
Inspire a new plan	Take the positive energy gained from opening up to feedback and others' sharing with you to work together to make your company a more awesome place.
Take charge of growing yourself and your culture	Start putting everything together toward a new way of being, with support from others. Learn about common Culture Stressors and how to turn things around with Culture Cultivators. Engage Culture Guardians.

What types of things will you observe when you WATCH IT? Essentially, you will notice behaviors—often strengths that are so strong, they've become weaknesses—that impact a group, function, the organization, or the entire culture depending on the influence, reach and position of the leader.

Ready? Let's dig in!

Walk Around

At first, you may wonder, "I've been here every day for the last several years, how can I see anything new? Where would I begin?" Great questions! I'll walk you through some things to look at and look for, so you'll be able to see your company with fresh eyes. This is what's going to make learning about your culture so interesting.

As you walk around, four areas to observe are (1) physical space; (2) communications; (3) employee experience; and (4) group dynamics. You can download the corresponding checklists from www.apowerfulculture.com.

For each area, jot down what you observe and give it a thumbs up or thumbs down. I created a thumbs up, thumbs down rating system to make it simple. The idea is to give a quick rating, not to get bogged down or caught up with numbers and data.

You may think, "But aren't there so many other things to explore in addition to the physical space, communications, employee experience and group dynamics?" Certainly. These four areas are a starting point. As you widen and deepen your research on your company culture, you will identify other areas into which to delve. As a lifelong learner who wants to maintain a fit, productive and sustainable organization, you can add items to the list for future review.

At this time, however, you will have plenty of exciting, eye-opening exploration and discovery opportunities within these four areas. Remember to take this one step at a time and know that with persistence and involving others you will learn more about what is going great and what can be done to make things better. Take a notepad, take some time and let the exploring begin!

TABLE 5. Physical Space Checklist

Supports viewing the physical environment and noting first impressions regarding space, employee behaviors and customer responses.

You can download the complete checklist from www.apowerfulculture.com. *The checklist will include columns for observations, initial assessments and potential solutions.*

Physical Space Checklist
1. Entrance What do you see in the front area and lobby? What impression does the furniture, frames, company information and seating make on you?
2. Behavior of Employees What do you observe in the employees who first interact with visitors or requests? Do they seem stressed/relaxed, friendly/unfriendly, neutral/uninterested, helpful/unhelpful?
3. Customer Area What does the customer waiting area look like? Is it neat? Is there a coffee or tea station or snacks? Is there reading material on the company or industry? Is there a monitor playing videos? If so, what is playing? Is the furniture nice or shabby? Are the floors and walls clean?
4. Office Design and Furniture Once you enter the office, what do you see? How is the furniture set up? Are there offices around the perimeters that have natural light? Are there cubicles and are they open or closed, modern or traditional?
5. Lighting How much natural light is in the office? Is the office bright or a bit dark?
6. On the Walls What do you observe on the walls? Are there memos, reminders of events, guidelines for behavior, customer testimonials, company values, art, etc.? How do these communications make you feel? Does it seem like an enjoyable or restrictive place to work?
7. Common Spaces What do you observe in the meal areas, conference rooms, break rooms and quiet rooms? Are they clean or dirty? Neat or messy? Tight or spacious? Is this a place you'd like to spend your time?

8. Dress Code

How do you observe the way employees are dressed? Is it formal, business casual, or casual?

Are people wearing clothes with the company logo?

Do they seem comfortable in the way they are dressed?

Does it look professional, semi-professional, or weekend casual?

9. Desks

Do the desks look modern, traditional, shabby, comfortable, or uncomfortable?

Are they private or open?

Overall, are the desks neat or messy? Are they sparse or decorated with personal effects such as pictures, customer notes, etc.

Are there plants or awards?

10. Pets

Are there pets in the office? If so, are they contained and staying in one area or are they roaming about?

What effect do the pets seem to have on staff? Are they pleased, neutral, or displeased?

11. Food and Beverages

Are food and drinks available to employees? If so, what kinds?

Healthy or less healthy options? Is there a mix?

What do you see in the break rooms, the front areas and the conference rooms?

When food is catered, what type of food is ordered? Do employees seem pleased?

What beverages are provided? Is there coffee, tea, or alcohol?

If there is alcohol, what types of guidelines (explicit and implicit) are there for consumption?

What times of the day do you observe employees drinking alcohol?

Who is drinking it (leaders, employees or both)?

12. Engaging Areas

Are there areas for employees to relax, have fun, or get creative?

What do they look like? Are they being used?

Who seems to be using them the most (leaders, employees, or both; specific demographic groups, etc.)?

13. Office Vibe

Is the office quiet, lively, loud or a mix depending on the area or time?

What are people talking about?

Do they seem relaxed or tense?

Does this seem like an extroverted or introverted space?

TABLE 6. Communications Checklist

Aids in observing how people are communicating with one another.

You can download the complete checklist from www.apowerfulculture.com. The checklist will include columns for observations, initial assessments and potential solutions.

Communications Checklist

1. Day-to-day Interactions

How do people talk with one another? Serious/joking, rushed/languid, joyful/terse, formal/casual, positive/negative?

2. Discussions Within Meetings

(Review this holistically and per department if possible.)

What is the meeting frequency (too often/not enough)?

Who runs them (manager/shared among the team)?

What is the focus (status/problem-solving/innovation)?

How structured or loose are the meetings? Are there agendas?

Is it all business? Is there informality/joking?

What is the engagement level?

Who is speaking? Men/women, extroverts/introverts, leaders with power, a facilitator, etc.? Are all staff involved?

Are people interrupting others? If so, what is the pattern, who is interrupting whom?

Is there an effort to be inclusive to everyone in the room and to hear all voices? If so, how do you know the group is being inclusive?

Are the ideas of men/women, minorities, extroverts/introverts, leaders with power/ staff acknowledged and valued?

Do meetings start and end on time?

Are there objectives at the end with accountabilities? What about the actions from the last meeting?

Do managers complain about back-to-back meetings with no time to do their work?

3. Virtual Meetings

Who shows up?

Is it mandatory for cameras to be on?

Are there small group discussions?

Does the communication feel one-way or two-way?

How do people feel when they leave the meetings? (Ask them.)

What is the level of engagement, joy and participation?

4. Messages from the Top

(Review the last three messages from your president or CEO.)

What are the main areas of focus?

What is the tone?

How do you feel after reading the communication (hopeless/hopeful, uninspired/inspired, curious/bored, etc.)?

Is there reference to the vision, values and strategy?

Are there messages about wins or successes?

5. Interactions with Customers

How do people talk about customers? With/without respect, as if they are partners/a pain?

6. Giving Back

In what ways does your company support non-profits and charities?

Is it with the same group consistently, or are there a mix of organizations the company supports?

What types of organizations are supported? Whom do they benefit?

Are there fundraising drives and do employees participate?

Are employees given time off to volunteer with organizations they support?

7. Company Ethos and Direction

How often do people refer to the company's vision, strategy and values?

Do people refer to the company's values? Are the values used to guide decisions?

TABLE 7. Group Dynamics Checklist

Gives an opportunity to observe how people interact with one another throughout the organization, from the most senior levels, to management meetings, to day-to-day interactions. We are in an evolving landscape, and post-pandemic, the workplace has changed. Many companies are mostly virtual while some have a hybrid approach. Some companies will go back live in some capacity. We are looking at the dynamics from the time people log in and log out and, in some cases, walk in until they walk out.

You can download the complete checklist from www.apowerfulculture.com. The checklist will include columns for observations, initial assessments and potential solutions.

Group Dynamics Checklist

1. Working Hours

What are the norms for working hours? What time do people schedule virtual or live meetings?

When do people generally come in and leave?

Are there comments when people start or stop work earlier/later than others?

2. Meals

When in person, what are the norms for meals? (Do people generally bring in lunch, eat at the workplace cafeteria, or dine out?)

Are meals ever brought in? How often? For what occasions?

3. After Hours

Do people tend to get together virtually or in person, outside of work, or at all?

Does the company sponsor events for employee resource groups (ERGs) or non-profits?

4. Flexible Hours

Are people encouraged to work remotely?

Are flexible hours available to certain departments or for certain positions?

Are flexible hours seen as a norm or outside the norm?

This section has been designed to help you think about your workplace during the pandemic as well as post-pandemic.

5. Cross-Functional Leadership

How do the heads of the departments seem to get along? (Does there appear to be cooperation, or is there tension that shows up in meetings and project work?)

Do you see finger-pointing between departments or get a sense of collaboration?

6. Conflict

How is conflict generally handled at the organizational level (confronted/avoided/confronted with care)?

What types of conflicts do you observe?

Who is fighting with whom and about what?

Does the culture seem to have razor-sharp elbows where conflict is confronted, or is there false harmony where people are not willing to speak up?

Have you observed conflict handled gracefully?

By whom and in what circumstances?

7. Innovation

What innovation has been developed between departments?

Are there certain departments that are more innovative than others?

Are there ways that new ideas are encouraged from staff? How?

8. Senior Team

What is the makeup of the senior team (men/women, ethnicities, experience level, diversity, etc.)?

How are decisions made?

How well do they get along?

Do members seem to support one another?

9. President/CEO

How much credibility does this leader hold?

How often does she/he speak to the entire company?

What is his/her tone?

How much do people seem to trust them?

TABLE 8. Employee Experience Checklist
Helps in reviewing the company's talent management and talent development strategies.

You can download the complete checklist from www.apowerfulculture.com. The checklist will include columns for observations, initial assessments and potential solutions.

Employee Experience Checklist

1. Onboarding and Training

How is an employee onboarded?

Is the person's work area prepared with computer/passcodes and general desk necessities? Do virtual employees have the access and tools they need to get going?

Do any of the leaders introduce themselves to new staff and welcome them?

Is there any sort of tour of the facilities? Is there an overview of the company? If so, what does the employee learn about the company, strategy, history, vision, etc.?

2. Manager Development

Do managers receive training before they start managing others?

Is there any kind of in-house mentor program?

How is the time managers invest in coaching their team members measured?

3. Employee Development

Coaching: How often are managers expected to meet with employees?

Feedback: How often do employees receive formal feedback?

Reviews: How are performance reviews handled?

Do employees write self-evaluations?

Are there clear paths for different positions within the company?

4. Talent Development

Is there a process for reviewing all talent in the organization (identifying high potentials, strong performers and those who need coaching)?

Do high performers receive additional coaching and training opportunities?

5. Office Environment

When observing people in person and virtually, do employees seem to enjoy being at work?

How do people behave on Friday afternoons and Monday mornings?

What is the general energy and mood in the office?

6. Rewards

How are people rewarded? Individually/by department/as a whole or combination?

What are people recognized for? How often?

Ask, Seek, Explore

So, you've "walked around," and often had a "virtual walk" and noticed a few things. You may have been happily surprised to observe that many of your employees seem engaged. The tone in meetings may be productive and efficient, yet friendly. Maybe your place seems neat and organized. It's important to note the positive.

You may have also seen some things that can be improved. Maybe the lunch room looks shabby and could do with some furniture upgrades. Perhaps the snack options the company provides don't align with your health-focused values. For each of the areas that you believe can be better, jot down some suggestions.

As you review your notes, it's not uncommon to find that you may even be troubled by a few of your observations. You may have noticed that some stations in your manufacturing plant are out of order. Or that the two times you walked in through the front, the receptionist—your company's first point of contact to the outside world—has quickly ended a call on a personal cell phone. Maybe the president's email memos seem sterile and uninspiring. Maybe you've sat in on a couple of meetings and seen that people rarely refer to the company strategy, even though developing this was a collaborative effort and shared organization-wide. There may be some common challenges within the departments. You wonder how you'll ever get to all these items on your ever-growing list. You may be tempted to put this book down and take a break from this space full of seemingly difficult-to-resolve problems.

Take a deep breath and exhale. Throughout the rest of this book, I will show you how to break your findings down into step-by-step manageable goals and seek specific team input for each of these areas.

Initiating WATCH IT with a Partner

One way to learn about detailed nuances within these four categories for observation (or other areas within your company culture) is by speaking with team members. You may decide to bring on one or more partners—for example, your HR manager or department heads—to go through a specific checklist or all four of them. When you sit down with your colleague to discuss and/or compare notes, be aware that you may experience some surprises. First, they may have collected some data on the things you're looking into, whether an anecdotal collection of observations, case examples, or recent conversations. If you're working with your HR manager, they often serve as the heart of the organization, someone the employees turn to with their challenges and successes. Second, your team member may tell you, "I've been wanting to do this for a while. Remember we talked about this?" Perhaps the seed was planted then and *A Powerful Culture Starts with You* became the second nudge. Thank your partner and highlight the road ahead!

Third, if your HR partner or department head has a small staff, or is under-staffed and worried about the time investment needed for examining and improving your culture, please put their concerns to rest. If you are starting with you, you can let them know that, "Working on our culture will be a partnership between me and critical stakeholder partners like you. It's important for the process that I be involved and this is a coordinated team effort, not just something that heavily rests on your shoulders without support. Do you have any suggestions on how to do this?"

Once you have your lists of observations from the four areas, you can work on a plan to do some reality testing around this. There are many ways to seek more information on your observations and hypotheses. You can:

1. Give the four checklists to a sample of formal leaders, informal leaders and employees. Your HR partner can help you select the group. Tell each person that these are just observations at this point and they can help you go deeper at a later time.
2. Set up focus groups and engage a trained facilitator to ask employees for their thoughts.
3. Create an online survey.
4. Go old school and provide a suggestion box. You may consider creating boxes for the different categories to get people's minds churning. Perhaps offer prizes for the top three suggestions.

Take in Feedback

Taking on the journey of seeking feedback is a big decision, one that can transform your organization, one area at a time. Do know two key things about seeking input: First, the very acts of seeking information and asking questions are the beginning of initiating the change process. It gets everyone thinking and creates momentum. Energy begets energy. Action begets action. Second, by seeking input, you are signaling that you plan on making change. So, it is important to report back to everyone the themes of the feedback and to actually make some changes.

How to Manage Feeling Overwhelmed

You may be thinking, "This sounds like a big process. How long will this take? Am I qualified to do this?" Depending on what you've observed of your culture, this may be a short process that gives you a snapshot of your culture and some actions you can take now. If you see a lot of room for improvement, you may want to partner with an organization development (OD) expert who can help you make improvements. Perhaps you will choose two areas to work on where you can create positive change (see Inspire a New Plan, p.45). If you choose carefully, gain supporters and follow through, you will gain confidence to make other changes.

And you are qualified to make many of the changes! This includes, but is not limited to, updating the office space, ensuring your talent development is robust by hiring the right HR partner, improving customer service by assembling a strong internal team to review the customer experience, providing healthier food for your people and so on. Each of these tasks, however large or small, is a positive change that leaves your culture stronger than before.

The determined driver that you are, you are probably chomping at the bit to do everything. Take a step back, take a deep breath and work on one area at a time. One of my favorite phrases is *Petit à petit l'oiseau fait son nid*—which, loosely translated from French, means bit by bit, the bird builds its nest. This philosophy guides my life, because I, too, want everything done as quickly as possible. I've come to learn that much of the learning, joy and wisdom come from the process, especially when it is slower than I would like.

Some Areas Will Be Harder than Others

Certain areas of making change will be easy and manageable while other areas will be difficult to approach. You'll examine the issue from different angles and find yourself frustrated at times. "Why can't I figure this out? Why is this so difficult?" I expect some frustration to come up; here are some reasons why:

1. *Too close for comfort*. You may be too close to a challenge, whether an interpersonal conflict, a disagreement about strategy, or an evolving group dynamic that is not working. The best route is to bring on a neutral facilitator or OD professional to help deconstruct and rebuild what you wish to improve.

2. *Lack of training.* You may not have the training required to drive some individual-based or team- or systems-related change. Why would you? You have your own special set of skills. And you can use this to help drive change when you partner with a professional who has been trained in culture development.

3. *You are part of the problem.* There may be a chance that you are part of the problem. In this situation, which is both common and okay (it is what it is; we need to start somewhere), you can benefit by engaging a coach who will help you to view your leadership and its impact on the culture in a new way and to clarify what's important. With support, you can create a vision for a preferred future and work on your goals.

Go Deeper: More Ways to Take in Feedback

If you have reviewed the four checklists, perhaps conducted focus groups and engagement surveys and even created a suggestion box, you may be wondering how else you can take in feedback. Conducting "stay interviews" is a way to learn why people stay at your company. You can begin by speaking with a sample of high performers about why they choose to stay with the company. Train your interviewers to ask the same set of questions and to carefully track the responses. Code the data and look for themes that emerge.

You can also seek counsel from your Culture Guardians—employees who care deeply for the company and are committed enough to risk giving you honest feedback. These are your scouts, eyes and ears on the ground, cheerleaders and problem-solvers. These are the team members who feel safe enough to tell you their concerns about the company. They are caring and conscientious and observe group dynamics like a hawk. Ask these people what you should be examining. Sometimes you don't know what you don't know.

Culture Guardians

Employees who care deeply for the company and are committed enough to risk giving you honest feedback. These are your scouts; your eyes and ears on the ground; your cheerleaders and problem-solvers.

Seek feedback with a focus on your diverse employee populations. For example, if you want to learn how the women in your company view the development and growth opportunities available to them, select a sample of women leaders, high performers and Culture Guardians. Ask them what's been going on and what they need for their development. For your own inner work, take time to examine if there may be any unconscious bias in the way your organization promoted women in the past.

Clarify and Understand

During the process of receiving feedback, you may experience an assortment of thoughts and feelings. Anything from, "I know that! Obvious!" to, "I have an idea of what they're talking about, fair enough"; or, "I have no idea what they're talking about, but I'm willing to explore it," all the way to, "They're full of crap. Period."

The Johari Window,[16] a model with four feedback zones, is a great tool that I share with clients to prepare them to receive 360-degree feedback. (This step comes after I've read reports; talked with the individual, their peers and supervisors; and have learned about the person's strengths and potential areas for improvement.) When it comes to clarifying feedback, the Johari Window can help you see what things you are aware of, what others are aware of and what areas may be blind spots. The four feedback quadrants are:

> *Open:* Information that you and others know. "I knew that and hearing Jay's comments confirmed it for me."

> *Hidden:* Things you know that others may not be aware of. "Perhaps I can share this part of my style with my team leads."

> *Blind spot:* Things others know that you are not aware of. "Oh, wow, I hadn't realized that! I'll pay more attention going forward."

> *Unknown:* Information that isn't known to you or others. "You don't know; I don't know."

....

16.   Joseph Luft and Harrington Ingham, "The Johari window, a graphic model of interpersonal awareness," *Proceedings of the Western Training Laboratory in Group Development* (Los Angeles, CA: University of California, Los Angeles, 1995).

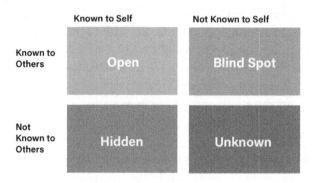

The Johari Window

Just being aware of these feedback zones will remind you that seeking feedback regularly can shine a spotlight on what you may not be aware of, strengths as well as suggestions. You will hear feedback that you're pleased with, some things that you disagree on and some information that's news to you. As you seek to understand other viewpoints, remember that your openness to the feedback (positive, negative and everything in between) is critical.

Note that I didn't say openness to *accepting and implementing all the feedback*. This is about openness to *hearing* feedback, showing appreciation for the effort and seeking clarification: "Tell me more," and "Can you help me understand?" If people sense your disapproval or discomfort with the input, they will quickly retreat while silently cursing themselves, "I knew I should have kept my mouth shut!"

The Johari Window is a tool to better understand your relationship with yourself and others; how others see your company culture, your teams and even your leadership. When you seek feedback regularly and receive it openly, you are also role-modeling this behavior and creating a feedback-rich culture, where employees feel comfortable sharing their thoughts, including about what can be better. A feedback-poor culture, by contrast, is where employees fear sharing their thoughts, leading to persisting problems that get worse as the months go on and ultimately impact your bottom line, customer service and employee engagement.

I encourage you to hold your views and assumptions lightly—even before seeking feedback. The more open and curious you are, the more you will be able to see. You will be less reactive and more likely to question your own assumptions—ultimately getting you closer to the truth and reality versus dreaming up worst-case scenarios and imagined meanings.

How to Manage Your Internal Reactions to Feedback

As helpful as it is to be polished, centered and calm on the outside as you receive feedback that you may initially be vehemently opposed to, it's just as important to be calm on the inside and not go into a negativity spiral. Managing your internal reactions is a big part of receiving feedback. The point is that we jump to conclusions based on little evidence. We need to be still long enough to let the feedback digest. Yet we jump to a negative assumption.

When we hear news that is unexpected or that we disagree with, we can get defensive, make up stories, assign meanings and even conclude that "this whole thing was a royal waste of time." The *ladder of inference*, a concept first developed by Chris Argyris,[17] describes a thinking process that happens, often subconsciously, to get from a fact or event to a decision or action.

At the bottom of the ladder of inference, we have data: *reality and facts*. We experience these through the filter of our beliefs and previous experiences and make an *interpretation*. We then layer on our existing *assumptions* over that interpretation, draw *conclusions* and form *beliefs* based on these conclusions. We *act* based on these beliefs and conclude that these actions are subsequently "right."

We can use this concept to examine our thinking in order to prevent making assumptions, which can lead to incorrect or poor decision-making and less effective outcomes. Let's say one of your Culture Guardians tells you she reviewed some recent customer feedback and saw that two customers said they had to call several times to receive the updates they needed. What happens next? If you're making assumptions and moving quickly up the ladder of inference, things might go something like this (read from bottom to top, working from reality and facts up to actions):

. . . .

17. Chris Argyris, *Overcoming Organizational Defenses: Facilitating Organizational Learning*, 1st ed. (Pearson Education, Inc., 1990).

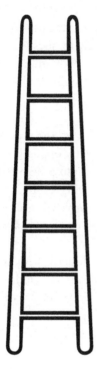

Actions

Holding an all-hands meeting, which employees later question and are unclear about.

Beliefs

"We need an all-hands meeting to explain the importance of customer care, our top value, to our staff and re-engage them on this value."

Conclusions

"Employees must be disengaged if they are acting like this."

Assumptions

"Our value of customer care doesn't matter to staff."

Interpreted reality

"We are not caring for customers."

Selected reality

"This must be a pattern."

Reality and facts

Your Culture Guardian told you two clients gave feedback on a lack of updates.

The Ladder of Inference

Something like this example can happen easily when we are inundated with data and trying to put out fires quickly. One piece of data from one employee snowballs into a big action that can reverberate negativity and fear throughout the organization. Ideally, you would stick with the facts, go slowly, investigate the situation to learn what happened and then coach the person on their follow-up. This would mean staying around the bottom of the ladder:

Actions

You follow up with a curious mindset and learn that it was an isolated incident. You coach the person and collaborate to create a new methodology so that the problem does not occur again.

Reality and facts

Your Culture Guardian told you two clients gave feedback on a lack of updates.

The idea is to stay longer in inquiry mode where you take things at face value without jumping to universal judgments. What if you learned that one of your best customer service advisors had been out unexpectedly and had forgotten to turn on auto-reply for emails, leading to the two customers not hearing back on their updates?

These types of inferences happen every day, whether about a conflict or someone's performance. When you choose to pause and investigate, clarify and understand, you can save yourself and others a whole lot of unnecessary grief. Plus, you role-model for others how to take in feedback.

Handle Your Ego

We need to understand the ego and do the work to notice when it is driving us, versus our driving it. When you receive feedback that's contrary to how you see the company, your ego, that pesky inner voice, may clap back with: "These employees are ungrateful … entitled. What does this team know about the realities of running a company? Their comments are bulls——t!" These negative messages, driven by your ego, will get you nowhere. In fact, they will cause more damage. The reality is no culture is perfect, and if you can learn how to handle your ego, you will be able to receive feedback with curiosity, grace and presence.

What is ego? One way of thinking about ego is that it's a part of the mind that tries to protect you from danger—which is great, for the times in our lives when we may be in danger and need to know if we should be in fight-or-flight or freeze mode. But since we rarely need it for purposes of true survival, as we are no longer running from large animals who want to eat us, the ego believes many other mundane things should be monitored regularly.

In ego's attempt to keep us safe, it sees seemingly neutral events as threats and ends up warning us about everything around us. This results in the mind staying hypervigilant for "safety reasons." But ego often does the opposite of protecting us from pain, despite its best efforts. When we listen to negative messages from our ego telling us that our colleague is trying to damage our reputation, or that our fellow board member thinks our ideas are naïve, or that our employee's input about the company culture is ill-informed, we end up feeling negative, distraught, angry, agitated and worried about outcomes that will likely never materialize.

What if we no longer need this incessant chatter about how the world is messed up and how people are out to ruin us? The ego still wants to feel needed and important. One way it does this is by keeping you stuck in the past, replaying old wounds and possible errors. Another way ego can stay employed is by making you anxious about the future—things that have never happened.

"But I'm just a troubleshooter trying to help." Ego.

If you achieve peace of mind and stability in the present moment, your ego will be unemployed!

Ego regularly sends us messages such as:

- You're in danger.
- You messed up.
- They messed up.
- You're not good enough.
- Things are going to fall apart.
- The future is dim.
- Watch out for them! They're out to make you look bad.

The ego creates separateness—and trouble—as it works hard to maintain a separate identity. Its logic dictates, "In order to protect my separate identity, I need to have something to protect." Ego needs to define itself by creating stories and making meaning out of day-to-day events. How does ego do this? Through defending itself from perceived attacks from invisible enemies. It also scans for threats and competition from the separate identities of others (other people's egos).

All. Day. Long.

Are you tired yet?

Doesn't just hearing about ego's job—sending our mind running around, acting like it's always under attack—sound exhausting? This is what keeps us from inner peace, self-love and stronger connections with others. It's what keeps us from being open to feedback. It's what makes us judge others and fear that they are judging us in return.

Step aside, ego! Four steps to peace:

1. Listen for the messages from your brain. (You messed up again!)
2. Are they helpful or hurtful? (Hurtful.)
3. Name the thought and fear. (You will fail.)
4. When the thought comes back, thank ego and shoo it away. (I'm doing the best I can with what I know. I will succeed. Thank you, ego. I've got this!)

Turn around Ego Responses

Ego serves as a troubleshooter that, like a security camera, scans the environment for danger and threats to our well-being. It tries to help us, warn us of perceived threats and defend us at all costs. But if ego goes unchecked, it wreaks serious havoc! And, by the way, ego running rampant is something we all deal with, all the time.—Unless you're one of the few who has worked hard to notice ego driving your thoughts, named what was happening and switched gears toward being in the present moment. If you're still on the path to that place of quiet peace, read on to learn how ego causes us to lose our inner joy and what you can do in the short and long term to identify and check ego for the purpose of creating total peace.

Handling your ego is key to having an open mindset to hearing feedback from your employees and colleagues about company culture, teams and individual leaders. Following are four common ways the ego is in self-defense mode to protect you. The more familiar you are with these common responses, the easier it will be to breathe it out, pause and reflect further on difficult feedback before responding.

1. ***It's not me; it's them.*** Our ego keeps us separate from the world by convincing us to point out others' flaws. "There's something wrong with her." "It's just that they're ungrateful." This keeps us feeling superior and better about ourselves, at least temporarily. Here's the kicker: the things your ego points out as undesirable in others are often projections of qualities you dislike in yourself. If you think, "My coworker isn't great with deadlines," it may be that you're unhappy with how you handle deadlines. "He can be so self-serving" may be more about your worries of being too self-focused in your work life. Don't feel bad, we've all done this—and will continue to do it until we develop awareness of this factor.

   Once you have this awareness and realize that your thoughts are judging someone else, you can ask yourself some questions: What is it about this issue that bugs me? Do I possess some of this quality or behavior? What would it look like if I worked on this?

   Turn it around: "Maybe there are some nuggets of truth I can learn from this. It's not an all-or-nothing deal. I can do some reality testing to see what others think. Let me shake it off and start working on a plan."

   Ego is a mirage. It's not you. It wants you to avoid danger, which includes perceived pain and shame. If you recognize how its messages keep you from being open to growth, you can stop it and become free.

2. ***I know better than you.*** The ego constantly checks how it compares to others, so it can create and maintain a positive image of itself. "I have way more experience than you. What do you know?" The ego wants to make sure you (and it) are safe and looking good. It wants you to feel that you're better than others, be that your competition, colleagues, neighbors or whoever else is a potential threat. It thinks in a black-and-white way of good versus bad, right versus wrong, them versus us and winning versus losing. Since the ego wants you to feel good and safe, it avoids what may be realities: that there are any number of shades of gray. If your ego judges you for being less skillful and intelligent than your competitor, it will cause you shame, pain and feeling inferior. This is the type of storytelling and meaning-making that can lead to a negativity spiral.

Turn it around: "Maybe this person is onto something. I value new ideas, so I'm going to stay open. I can do this!" This may be a chance to test your own biases. Notice if you are resisting feedback from certain audiences such as women, people of color, people who are less experienced, people who are extroverted, people who are from a different generation, etc.

"Not me," you say, "I'm open to everyone." We all think we don't have biases … but we all have them. It's human nature. It comes from how we've been raised, the communities we've lived in, the behaviors that have been rewarded, the places we work, the social media we follow. It goes on and on. The point is to notice our behaviors and learn to identify patterns in our responses.

3. *It's not my fault.* The twin of "I'm better than you," this defense mechanism leads to avoiding responsibility, because it makes you feel guilt and shame, the last things ego wants to feel and will avoid at all costs.— Even if it means throwing coworkers under the bus and assigning blame or denying you're part of the problem so you can maintain your constructed positive image to the world. The thing is, not only do you become the person who is known for pointing the finger or shifting blame and not only does your team suffer but you also end up looking bad in the long run anyway. When you feel your defensiveness rising up—ego coming on strong to defend you, often before you have even heard the whole story—take a pause. Breathe and listen. Decide you won't respond until you have all the facts and time to digest them. Ego, left to its own devices, without a pause and space, will make you attack others and be the person you don't want to be.

Turn it around: Ask yourself if the "it's not my fault" response is a pattern in other areas of your life. Do you shirk blame, because the feedback, which may be truth, makes you feel bad? It would help to explore the root of these feelings. For now, perhaps you can find comfort in knowing that you have power to drive a great team environment. Accountability is a decision and it's empowering to remove the blame element and think of how much power you have to turn things around. Celebrate that, as a leader, it starts with you.

4. ***Don't I look good?*** Since our ego sees itself as a separate entity, it needs to ensure that it's always seen in the best light. Granted, managing one's executive presence is a healthy way of knowing when to be a bit more buttoned up, articulate and professional. This type of impression management can gain you respect, employment and likeability—all important for connecting with your audience. What I'm talking about here is how you present in real life, in your conversations and among your teams. If you're in "looking good" mode, you may talk more than you listen; you may unintentionally brag or pull all the attention toward yourself and how great you are. After a while, this type of looking "good" and presenting a "positive" image may come across as self-absorbed and uninterested in others. You may not even be aware you're doing it. Here are some questions you can ask yourself or use to get feedback: How much do I talk and how much do I listen? If I'm talking about my new car or the trip I'm planning, am I aware of my audience and those around me who may not have the time or means for such things? Do I interrupt others? Do I turn people's stories into a story about my experiences?

    Turn it around: Your ego seeks approval for the image it projects into the world. What if you were to accept the fact that change can be messy and require a team? By sharing this truth with your team as you drive change, you take the pressure off yourself to look perfect. Use this change process as an opportunity to make others feel good about their strengths and accomplishments.

There are many ways our ego impacts our behavior and how we show up and operate in the world. These are just a few of the ways ego can get ahead of us, stress us out, hurt our relationships and ultimately keep us from being our best selves, authentic, joyful and connected in the world— and how we can turn things around. Understanding what the ego is, what it does and how you can manage it, in order to tap into your best, most authentic self at work, home and in your community is amazing, deep work that can change your life.

The Masks We Wear When Ego Is in Overdrive

Have you ever met someone with such a distinguishing behavior or personality trait—like so nice, so mean, so much joking around—that you come to experience them as over the top or even exhausting? Agreeable Guy is so overly agreeable that it makes you wonder, "Are you really okay with everything?" Tough Gal expresses nothing but toughness, so you think, "Does anything ever meet your standards?" The office joker makes light of so many things that you wonder, "Do you ever take anything seriously?"

When people have extreme behaviors, it is likely that ego has become over-protective, taking over parts of their personalities or lives. If left unchecked, ego can become so extreme that a quirk in our behavior or something to pay attention to, like, "I need to keep stories focused on others," or, "I'm going to work on more internal validation," turns into a full-on mask. Common masks we wear include Mr. Nice Person, Ms. Perfect, Mx. Self-Righteous; M. Happy Hour and so on. I'm sure you can think of several others.

How does this happen? When we get rewarded for certain behaviors, often starting from childhood, we repeat those behaviors. The child who was always told to "be good and help everyone" will usually grow up into a nice person who considers the feelings of others or always goes out of their way to help. As you understand more about the ego, how it wants to protect us and how overprotection can turn into a mask, you may see that we can be trapped in our own minds and kept from our own greatness. Anxiety acts as a signal to the ego that things are not going the way ego wants. As a result, the ego then employs some sort of defense mechanism to help reduce these feelings of anxiety. You may remember hearing about defense mechanisms, including those that come up in day-to-day conversation like, "He's in denial," or, "They're acting out."

If you're thinking, "Geez, the ego is a tricky thing!"—absolutely correct. Working on combatting all the "stuff" the ego tells us is hard work. It can be confusing, ambiguous and headache-inducing. It is lifelong work to become aware of the negative messages ego sends and to turn them around. In the moment, it requires taking a deep breath, thanking the ego for its "assistance," and coming up with more positive ways of looking at a situation. This takes attention, time and practice.

The process requires you to suspend judgment (including of yourself) and to question your automatic defenses and assumptions. It requires pausing before reacting. It may help to seek feedback from a few people you trust. You can also equip yourself with more knowledge about the ego, how it works and how to control it. You may also need to be in a good space in your life to more deeply examine how you show up in the world, how you interpret others' words and the masks you may don to gain esteem from others. When you're ready, these reflection questions may aid you in exploring the roots of what triggers your ego responses.

Reflection: Exploring Ego Triggers

1. What messages did I grow up with about myself, relationships, the world?
2. Might I be wearing any masks?
3. Might I be employing any defense mechanisms to my detriment?
4. How do I normally take feedback?
5. Have I ever received feedback that I'm not open to?
6. How can I not take the feedback personally?

Benefits of Deep Work

Working on recognizing your ego and the ways it hurts you is deep work—with life-changing benefits. Here's what you stand to gain:

1. You'll be okay with your own and others' flaws. You will have more self-love and love for others.
2. You'll realize that we're all on our own paths, doing our best. You won't feel compelled to keep proving to yourself and others that you're better than anyone.

3. You'll be open to taking accountability and receiving feedback in areas where you can do better. When you tell others what you're working on, they'll appreciate your growth mindset and transparency.

4. You'll have the space to be fully present when talking with others, able to immerse yourself in another's world. You'll be curious and collaborative, asking questions to learn more. There will be an absence of a need to prove yourself and your worth by highlighting your stories.

5. You'll experience less drama, because you'll be pausing to understand feedback. You won't jump to conclusions or to defend yourself.

6. You'll be free and your ego will be out of business.

Inspire a New Plan

There are ways to inspire a new plan that can propel positive momentum toward a needed change. Appreciative inquiry (AI), created by David Cooperrider and Suresh Srivasta, centers on "the search for the best in people, their organizations and the strengths-filled, opportunity-rich world around them."[18] Appreciative inquiry is about looking for what works well in a system—learning about the strengths, successes and possibilities—rather than focusing on problems and challenges.

Four processes of appreciative inquiry are:

1. **Discover** the best of what is.
2. **Dream** what could be.
3. **Design** what should be.
4. **Deliver** what we will do.

Mukhtar, a co-project manager for a construction firm, wanted to learn why his sales team was having a lower percentage of their proposals accepted. The team of five felt discouraged about their decreased success. I used AI concepts to engage Mukhtar's team in describing five wins they'd had. What was happening when they were preparing for those meetings? How did each person contribute? What was the vibe from the start to finish? What happened when there were client questions or changes? I asked them to speak with the clients from these five successes to learn what went well with those

---

18. Jacqueline Stavros, Lindsey Godwin and David Cooperrider, "Appreciative Inquiry: Organization Development and the Strengths Revolution," in *Practicing Organization Development: A Guide to Leading Change and Transformation*, 4th ed., ed. William Rothwell, Roland Sullivan and Jacqueline Stavros (Wiley, 2015).

presentations and what the clients had observed about the team's interactions during those times. The team had some interesting information to share at our next meeting.

Jay, Mukhtar's co-project manager, shared, "That was an eye-opening exercise. We were all in a more gracious space with each other during those wins. Even though we had little mess-ups here and there before submitting the proposals to clients, we were positive and not finger-pointing. We gelled as a group and covered for each other to fix things. During those projects when we were thriving and winning, we were having lunch as a team a couple of times a week. We were riding one high after another, because we were on a roll! We felt unstoppable!"

Mukhtar added, "The clients we spoke with said they enjoyed the rapport they had with team members and the frequency of touch-base calls. One client said the team's energy was infectious and that we seemed to enjoy working together."

As each team member shared their findings, there seemed to be both an electricity and stillness in the air. After they all shared similar findings, everyone sat in silence for a moment.

Jay sat up suddenly. "Guys, we let our good vibes go! We got lost in the busyness of it all. When was the last time we had lunch together? And we've all been so tense. I know I played the blame game last week, I'm sorry. We can turn this around!" The team smiled. I could hear what sounded like sighs of relief.

I brainstormed some turnaround actions with the team in areas they identified, including team presence, client connection, fearlessness and grace. They recommitted to team lunches weekly and came up with fun ways to keep their spirits up. A few weeks later, I received a text from Mukhtar, "We got our mojo back! I believe it's what led to our recent big win!"

Tap into the Group's Wisdom

Dr. Leena, a client in the healthcare industry, said that her team seemed stuck, doing things the same way over and over. Their meetings were disengaging; people showed up late and then worked on their laptops. The effort seemed lackluster as did the results. "I wonder what we're doing here," Dr. Leena said. "It's a bunch of bodies but no one is connecting."

I suggested that instead of viewing the situation as a big problem needing a major overhaul and requiring a large investment of time and energy, why not consider initiating a mini-experiment? The team could identify a challenge, deliberate on solutions, pick one to try, see what worked and what didn't and then revise it. The cycle (referred to as action planning) can continue as the team learns in action until the group is satisfied with the outcomes.

I met privately with the eight team members to discuss what they thought was going well with the meetings and what wasn't working. The overwhelming response was that the meeting was a boring status update that could be done over email; there was no social element to it and no one cared if you were on your laptop. This was a smart group of people who weren't using their collective minds and experience to help one another. Tony, Dr. Leena's co-lead and such a fun personality, rolled his eyes as I asked how the meetings could improve, "¡Dios mío! These sessions are awful! I know this is what we don't want. I'm not sure what we do want yet."

After I shared some best practices for how a group can tap into its power, energy and collective wisdom, Dr. Leena and Tony proposed changing the meeting purpose to accomplish one of three things: solving problems; generating ideas; or coaching the group. A couple of people would have the chance to share a challenge; the group would ask questions and help create solutions. Tony asked one person to keep track of the project status and update everyone weekly.

The group met once a week for each of the three meeting purposes and closed the meeting by reflecting on what worked and giving suggestions. They applied the learnings to each new session. They later decided that the meetings were going so well, they wanted to have them every two weeks but for two hours so they could get the best out of their time together. They were so successful as a team that they started sharing their best practices with other departments.

Take Charge of Growing Yourself and Your Culture

I hope you have observed from the WATCH IT steps so far that culture is not some vague thing out there. It is a collection of behaviors by a group of people. Culture is the heart and soul of the company and changing it is in your hands.

An experienced coach can help you to better understand the assumptions, patterns, values and actions influencing your leadership. The International Coaching Federation (ICF) defines coaching as "partnering with clients in a thought-provoking and creative process that inspires them to maximize their personal and professional potential." Having this support from a qualified coach can be especially helpful around areas of feedback from your team that may be difficult for you to process at first. Changing things in your culture requires deep inner work that can help you discover who you want to be and what you want to stand for. Examples of feedback that may require deep reflection include:

1. You have a high-performing manager who is grumpy or even mean to your team. People have left because of this individual. You are torn on what to do.
2. Some employees' salaries are well below what is standard for your industry.
3. Your workplace feels unsafe, and appropriate safety standards are not always reinforced.
4. Your functional leaders squabble with one another and protect their turf.
5. There is a negative view of certain generations in the workplace.
6. Your company lacks diversity and does not seem to be inclusive of women and people of different cultures or genders.
7. Innovation among the departments seems impossible. Ignoring this results in the same repeated mistakes that cost time and money.

When these types of issues are neglected by a lack of response or leadership, they can grow from solvable challenges to Culture Stressors that negatively impact your work environment and staff engagement.

Culture Stressors: How Smart Leaders Damage Culture

Years of coaching and partnering with intelligent, insightful leaders have revealed some common mistakes and patterns, what I call Culture Stressors. Culture Stressors are leadership behaviors that stress the culture, demotivate people and frequently negatively impact revenue. There are many Culture Stressors that damage what leaders are trying to build and end up hurting company culture. I've seen that even smart leaders can unintentionally fall into these patterns. Often, it's connected to when a leader's top strength has been overused or overplayed to the point of being out of balance and subsequently has become a weakness. Culture Stressors become harder to solve the longer they go on. Whatever the behavior or dynamic that you or others don't like or find destructive or unhelpful, it doesn't have to be that way. You can change your culture, one step at a time.—*A Powerful Culture Starts with You!*

Patterns of Common Culture Stressors

Following are several case studies describing common Culture Stressors and foundational steps for change. The case studies cover examples ranging from the environment the leader creates, to how innovation and execution are balanced, to how the leader focuses on short-term versus long-term goals. I've categorized the patterns of common Culture Stressors into three thematic leadership styles: (1) head versus heart; (2) safety versus risk; and (3) today versus tomorrow. Each of these opposing styles has its strengths and challenges; the ideal is when leaders can balance several styles.

HEAD VERSUS HEART

Head is a strong, rational, direct style that may lack relationship-building leading to disengaged teams. Heart is an empathetic style that may lack the ability to hold people accountable, leading to poor performance.

SAFETY VERSUS RISK

These are two styles that companies need to create and execute innovation, but it can hurt the culture when they are extremely strong. The safety style can be risk-averse and resistant to needed changes. The high-risk style is invested in changing at a fast rate without prioritizing or managing change or its consequences.

TODAY VERSUS TOMORROW

These styles are about the leader's focus of energy. The today-style leader is agile and flexible, quickly responding to change and often resisting slowing down to focus on strategy. The tomorrow-style leader is organized and methodical to the point of resisting emerging information that can disrupt the perfect plan.

Patterns of Common Culture Stressors

The following case studies come from real-life clients I have worked with as a Master Certified Coach. I've done my best to share the examples with clarity while protecting client confidentiality and identity by using aliases, amalgamating related stories into a single example, or updating background information or the industry setting.

Most of these case studies reference using 360-degree feedback: a confidential process through which someone receives feedback from their superiors, peers, direct reports and sometimes even from clients and vendors. The benefit of 360-degree feedback is that it's an opportunity for a leader to see where people recognize their strengths as well as areas where skill and/or mindset development could be beneficial. Some high-driving leaders get antsy in their seats when you compliment their strengths and want to hurry on to the professional development areas, but creating the balance of acknowledging strengths is important because these can be channeled toward what needs to be changed.

The case studies reflect a few condensed interactions in the coaching process and perhaps some of the more important moments of self-reflection that the client experienced. There are no magic coaching questions (or magic coaches—including yours truly), but in these case studies, I've focused on the moments when clients have realized something key about themselves or their actions that needed to change. This reflects the client's openness to having a beginner's mindset and exploring their assumptions and interpretations. While it may seem like realization happens in a moment, implementing change takes time and consistent practice. Clients often experience months of trying new ways of being, falling back into old patterns, getting back up and trying again. There's no shortcut or substitute for doing the work.

Anyone who wants to do the work of learning; changing; and becoming stronger, more powerful, more intentional, more successful will experience a series of opportunities, options and decision points where they must choose. You will learn in each case study what is at stake for the client; the obstacles and flaws that exacerbate the situation—such as personality style, limiting beliefs, ego, blueprint—and the secondary gains that keep the person in their comfort zone. Rather than viewing any of these clients as difficult or challenging, I encourage you to see where their style is the power that has brought them results and where this style has become so strong—overplayed—that it is now a liability and danger to the culture.

Each person's work centers around adapting their style versus completely letting go of or changing their style, much of which works.

Each section concludes with an overview and a reflection. Read on and see which Culture Stressors speak to you, whether you relate or have seen leaders in your company who seem to have similar challenges. Here's to your equipping yourself with knowledge of common Culture Stressors and the tools to help drive strong, intentional mindsets and behaviors so you can strengthen your culture.

 HEAD VERSUS HEART

"It's Just Business" Hurts Business:
Capture Hearts and Loyalty Will Prevail

When attempting to create change in an organization, having relationships with those you need on board is essential. This goes beyond the perfunctory "How was your weekend?" check-in. I'm talking about the type of relationship where you know what matters to each person, personally and professionally. This is critical as you seek input about your vision for change and share why it is important for the organization, its people and customers.

Jack Roland was a director at a global manufacturing organization. He was witty, sharp and in your face. His strong personality went along with a strong work ethic. In his stern and direct style, he'd go into the office, give directions to others, do his work, follow up with his reports and go home.

He met me at the door of his office trailer. Jack was tall and fit, like a Nike mannequin. From our earlier conversation, I perceived him as someone who was serious, driven and dedicated. He welcomed me in and offered me coffee and water. Without any chitchat, he got right to it: "The people at this place treat me like a junkyard dog. They ignore me and I'm not sure how I'm supposed to make them change their ways. They run the site in such an outdated way that it delays our products getting to customers. How am I supposed to do my job with this situation?"

Okay then, I thought. Not surprised by his demeanor and straight-to-the-point style, I reminded myself to temporarily forget about the 360-degree feedback that corresponded with what I was seeing. I took in a deep breath so I could be fully present to understanding Jack's world.

Jack had been with the company for five years and successfully operated another location. Pritha, the chief executive officer (CEO), had asked him to relocate to this site to help update their procedures. The current site had performed fairly well with modest growth each year—until recently. Customers wanted more streamlined processes for making and tracking orders and they wanted to receive shipments more quickly.

The problem was that the culture at this site was much more relaxed than at the other sites. They were typically the last ones to implement new systems and processes. Faced with new technology and demands, it was getting difficult to keep up and please existing and new clients. Pritha decided to bring in a change agent who knew the organization and could improve efficiencies. If the leaders at this location were not going to get with the program, she was ready to get new players.

Enter Jack Roland. He was articulate, organized and ambitious. He had exceeded expectations thus far, so the senior executives thought he'd be a perfect fit to lift this team, transform the leaders and propel them from mediocrity to greatness.

As I listened to Jack's background and how he came to this site, I observed the inside of the trailer. With fading gray carpet and nondescript walls, it wasn't much to look at. There were no pictures or décor to speak of and I didn't see any frames on Jack's desk, which was adjacent to the eight-seater folding table where we were seated. Knowing that our environment can impact our mood and mental health, I thought a couple of plants could spruce up the place.

Sitting up straight at the end of the table, fingers interlaced, Jack looked at me intensely with his piercing blue eyes and said, "I've never experienced this type of behavior from employees before. It almost feels like they want me to fail."

I remained silent and nodded. Jack slumped slightly. Even though we had not yet opened Jack's feedback report, it felt like he sensed what was coming. As he spoke, his arms were crossed and his eyebrows knitted into a slight frown.

I circled back to his opening statement. "A junkyard dog?" I asked. "What does that mean and how does that show up?"

"Well, when employees see me, they may mumble a hello. No one really talks to me and I rarely get invited to lunches. I feel pretty isolated. I'm not having a good time here."

"I'm sorry to hear that, Jack. How does that make you feel?"

"Worthless and embarrassed. Unproductive, ultimately, because I'm not able to do what I came here to do."

"Let's review your feedback and see what we can learn," I suggested with a hopeful tone.

"Okay, let's take a look," he said as he slumped further down in his chair.

The positive feedback centered around his ability to understand the organization's different departments and how they all fit together. He was seen as strategic, bright and dedicated to the company. So far, so good.

"All right, Doc, give it to me. What was on their crap list? I'm ready."

Not wanting to admonish him or tell him to be more positive, I let the comment stand. I would give him space to process the feedback so he could determine if indeed it were "crap" or if there were enlightening clues he could use to turn this situation around. We started reviewing the developmental feedback:

> "He takes work seriously and rarely acknowledges us as humans with lives and families. It's a bit disconcerting."

> "He would benefit from getting to know his staff, who they are, what motivates them and where they want to grow."

> "We don't know Jack very well. He's efficient and does his thing, but he's a bit of a loner."

> "He is efficient in operating projects and aggressive at working toward deadlines, but there is something missing. People don't seem to connect with him."

We sat silently for a bit. He took a long breath in through his nose and let it out through his mouth, as if trying to blow out the negative energy and calm himself.

"Can you help me understand what they want from me? I bring bagels once a week. I'm clear with what everyone needs to do and I ask them if they need help. What more am I supposed to do?" he asked.

I leaned forward to demonstrate my support and mirror his serious tone. "It sounds like there are some things you are doing right. What are you taking away from the feedback comments?"

"I suppose they want more of my time. Do they want me to chitchat all day? That's not really me. I want everyone to do their best work. Let's be efficient and then move on to the next thing. How am I supposed to drive change in this environment? See what I mean?—Junkyard dog. I'm on my own, wading in the swamps. If there were any quicksand, I doubt anyone would help get me out."

"Those are some powerful metaphors you just shared. Can we unpack that a bit? First, help me understand the traits of a junkyard dog," I asked.

"A junkyard dog is neglected. This dog is mean, because he's unloved. I think at its core, maybe the dog just wants to be loved."

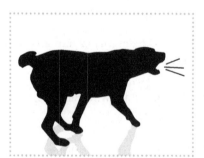

I looked at Jack and held the silence. What he shared was so powerful. He sounded like he was suffering. I got a glimpse of an emotional side as Jack rested his head in his hands.

"The dog just wants to be loved. Can you share more?"

He leaned back, arms still folded across his chest and stared out the window.

"Damn! I'm that dog who just wants love."

I wanted to jump up and down and say, "Yes, Jack, you get it! Go with this. Wanting love is a positive thing." I slowly nodded my head. "What might be possible if this dog were loved?" I asked.

"People would know I care. I've contributed to this. I'm so used to being efficient that I've neglected the human side of things. In my other location, everyone demonstrated the same style and put business first. Since we knew each other, it worked. Here, since they don't know me, it's like pulling teeth to get anyone to do anything."

"Everyone had the same style?" I asked.

"Well, now that I look back, I did tick some people off back then as well. Is there hope for me? I want to connect with people and make a big difference. I'm committed to this company and these people."

I shared my view that human potential is limitless, as long as there's an open mindset and desire to change. "What's your energy around doing the work, Jack?" I asked.

"I'm ready, Dr. Shahrzad! My energy is high. I need help taking the steps. I'm sure it'll be hard, but I want to try."

I asked him how he interacts with people during the day. It turned out that he didn't greet people, was serious at meetings and usually ate alone. In a way, he was creating a self-fulfilling prophecy—a prediction or expectation that affects behavior in a way that makes the prediction or expectation a reality—and people were reacting to him. Deep down, he did want to be liked, but for some reason, he was either stuck on what to do or had not discovered the importance of certain actions. He thought that all that chitchat and water cooler talk would eat up too much of his time and reduce efficiency.

He said he didn't feel interested in talking to so many people outside of work tasks. I shared with him Blake and Mouton's[19] managerial grid for how much a leader focuses on tasks, people and both; and the outcomes these styles tend to produce. By having a high concern for tasks and little concern for people,

19. Robert R. Blake and Jane Mouton, *The Managerial Grid: The Key to Leadership Excellence* (Houston, TX: Gulf Publishing Company, 1994).

his authoritarian style was getting him short-term results and preventing the real change he was seeking. But by getting to know everyone and building trust, he would get help in managing the change the site needed.

When I showed him Gallup's Q^{12} survey,[20] twelve questions that help determine how engaged and willing someone is to go above and beyond, he stated that if his people were asked these questions, they would give some low scores, particularly around his giving recognition and caring about them personally. "I'm getting some awareness right now about how I've been showing up. I have regrets. I was also doing my best." He stared at me for several seconds. "I've neglected nurturing my team."

"Can you think of someone who does a good job of ensuring a focus on tasks *and* people?"

"Terry Benedict, Andy Garcia's character in *Ocean's Eleven*.[21] He knew every staff member, their birthdays, anniversaries, kids' birthdays and major life events! I want to be like that."

I felt almost giddy looking at Jack's big smile. He got it! We high-fived at the huge connections he'd made and took a break before the goal-setting part of our session. During the break, Jack sent check-in emails to his team and thanked them for holding down the fort in his absence.

In the months following this session, Jack put in the work. He conducted regular check-in meetings, initiated lunches and invited everyone to share feedback as he made changes. Of course, he received love back from his team and often exclaimed, "Everyone has changed so much now! They're friendly and they even invite me to their events. This office is performing just as well as the other offices—in fact, we're going to surpass the other locations soon! My team needed some convincing and hand-holding through updating our systems, but the process was so worth it! We're increasing revenue every month. This feels like one of my biggest accomplishments—but it's *theirs*."

....

20. Gallup. "The Power of Gallup's Q12 Employee Engagement Survey," Gallup Access, Gallup, accessed October 11, 2021, https://www.gallup.com/access/323333/q12-employee-engagement-survey.aspx.

21. *Ocean's Eleven*, directed by Steven Soderburgh (2001; Warner Bros. Pictures).

SUMMARY

If you're a task-focused leader, organized and structured, you may do all the right things to move projects forward—except focus on the people. You may be so caught up in creating efficiency that you don't realize that creating change and an invigorating workplace culture takes as much effort as managing projects. Caring for and nurturing employees is a large part of building trust and growing the organization. It builds commitment and ownership and creates a positive energy that helps during tough times.

Leadership Style
Sterile, serious, task-focused, lack of positive emotion.

Result
Work is work; people do the work and go home.

Impact
Lack of commitment and ownership from your people, decreased bottom line, poor customer service.

Realization
Getting to know employees and chatting with them regularly is not a waste of time.

Examine Your Blueprint
Explore your mindset on your own and then with a trusted colleague or coach. Consider the origins of your leadership style and new ways of looking at it.

Examine Your Blueprint

Where did I learn this style of work?

_____

_____

_____

How is it helping me?

_____

_____

_____

Where is this preventing success?

_____

_____

_____

Whom have I observed with a task- and people-oriented style?

_____

_____

_____

How can focusing on relationships help me, my team, and my company grow?

_____

_____

_____

ACTION STEPS

- Walk around and talk to people several times a week when you are most relaxed. If your most productive work time is in the mornings, conduct your walking visits in the afternoons.
- Incorporate humor, inspiration and positivity into each meeting with stories, videos and real-life examples of how staff members have gone above and beyond to help clients and teammates.
- Read literature regularly on how to motivate and connect with staff.
- Create a coaching culture by asking people what they need help with. Ask the Q^{12} questions and practice staying calm even if you feel like becoming defensive. Be open, stay curious, ask follow-up questions and thank people for their input.

HEAD VERSUS HEART

False Harmony Gets You Nowhere:
Embrace Conflict and Liberate the Truth

Jack's experience shows how adding a more relationship-oriented approach to a very direct style gets results. On the other end of the continuum is a leader who focuses on harmony, group wellness and protecting the feelings of his team. It's a lovely style, until it becomes overplayed. If this type of leader does not pay attention to where their light becomes a shadow, they can become too indirect, which seems to minimize conflict but creates false harmony. Avoiding important conversations, particularly about performance, negatively impacts customer service, team dynamics and financial outcomes.

Dr. Jones had approached me for leadership coaching. "I just want my team to get along better and solve their daily issues. Some team members could be more productive. The managers seem to always come to me. I know I should spend my time growing the business. What should I do?"

Dr. Jones leaned forward as he spoke, making great eye contact and drawing me in. He had a warm smile. I guessed that his employees must enjoy working for him. He owned and operated a dozen medical offices. An entrepreneur at heart, he had developed amazing instructional videos that aired on local television and drew throngs of patients to his offices. His gentle manner appealed to the viewers who called and requested him specifically.

When we sat down for our first session, I asked Dr. Jones what he liked about the business. "I've grown it from one office. I love creating great experiences for our customers. I enjoy creating a nice workplace for people. I do like helping the office managers, because I am knowledgeable. Some of the office managers are tough, so sometimes I need to step in, but then I wonder if I shouldn't just let them handle things. I don't want to ruin the nice environment we've created. I'm afraid that if there's conflict, staff may become unhappy and leave. No one likes to hear arguments and debates. My vision is having a relaxing work environment where people are kind to one another."

"That sounds really nice. Can you share with me what you mean by 'ruin'?"

"I don't want conflict. I don't want people to get into fights. The strong personalities could create a lot of tension and then I'd need to come to the office more often."

"Share with me more about how you get involved."

"Well, for example, an employee will report an issue with the office manager and I'll come in to mediate. Things will get better for a while and then the same issue will arise again," he said.

"How would you like things to be?"

"In a perfect world, each of my office managers would manage the practice they're responsible for with few problems. They need to become better managers and hold people accountable, but in a kind way."

As we continued to talk, I discovered that Dr. Jones frequently intercepted his managers. On the one hand, he would tell them to manage the practice on their own. On the other hand, he would display "seagull syndrome"[22] and swoop down every so often to "make sure" the managers demonstrated a warm style.

Seagull Syndrome

refers to when an owner or executive tries to empower others, stepping back from the situation to give others the responsibility, but then returns, swooping down over them and changing back anything they don't like. Just as sailors get annoyed when seagulls swoop down and crap over the deck, making a mess of everything, employees may see owners who hesitate to give others control in the same way.[23]

"How is this working for you?" I asked.

Dr. Jones stood up and walked to the window with his hands in his pockets.

22. Ichak Adizes, *Managing Corporate Lifecycles* (Englewood Cliffs, New Jersey: Prentice Hall Press, 1999).
23. Robert A. Mines et al., "CEO/Owner/Founder Vulnerability: The Founder's Traps," BizPsych, October 24, 2011, https://minesandassociates.com/documents/The_Founders_Traps.pdf.

"Not well. But I don't want my office managers to scare people off with a harsh style. What do you think?"

"Has anyone left because of a manager's style?"

"No. Our people tend to stick around."

"What percent of your staff would you say contain A players—people qualified for the work, performing well and showing up with a great attitude?"

"If you put it that way, maybe 70 percent. Is that bad?" he asked, as he sat back down and put his head in his hand and started rubbing his temples.

"It's a good start and you obviously excel in many areas. You know how to market and how to scale; you role-model kindness—all admirable qualities. Do you mind if we look through your feedback to see what we could learn together?"

"Sure," he said and then more timidly, "Should I be nervous?"

"There are some very positive themes about what you're doing well. This work is about celebrating your strengths and then deciding what areas you'd like to work on. I know you have the answers for what you should work on. My job is to help you uncover that and support you as you take steps toward new behaviors."

"Okay, let's do this," he said, clapping his open hands to the table to punctuate his declaration. His mischievous smile told me he was ready to work. Perfect! I appreciated his energy (and, generally, I love these moments)!

The positive feedback highlighted a warm, considerate and employee-centered style:

> "He gives us all the tools we need and is always asking us if we feel satisfied."

> "When we experience an office conflict, he will come in and mediate for us."

"I feel really good working here. I feel cared for and I don't think I would easily find another place like this."

The areas to work on focused on being more direct and calling out the elephant in the room.

"We discuss ideas among ourselves for how to help the front office and back office work together better, but we feel afraid to bring them up, because the doctor gets uncomfortable when we debate about something. We could be more efficient and get along better if we could talk things out."

"He doesn't hold people accountable when they underperform in their work. He'll say, 'She's trying hard,' when the truth is that the person is not following up on her responsibilities."

"I wish he would clearly state what everyone needs to do and then let us hold the staff accountable for it. Although his style is nice, I don't think we get the best out of everyone."

"Well, what do you think?"

"I want to make sure people feel happy. I don't like having an argumentative culture. I think we need to treat people with respect," Dr. Jones said with passion and conviction.

"Absolutely! I'm on board with you. My question is: What if you coach someone and they continue to deliver poor work and have a poor attitude?"

"It's hard for me to let people go. The economy isn't good and I don't want the burden of making someone's life harder by firing them."

"I'm curious, what do you consider to be signs of commitment from your employees?"

"Keeping me updated and giving me ideas for how to run things more efficiently. Great at mediating issues with patients and staff. Those are probably what you called my A players."

"How does it feel to have A players?"

"So good, Dr. Shahrzad! It gives me pride that they care so much."

"Tell me about the rest of your players. What does their commitment look like?"

"Well, you met one of my teams last week. What did you observe?"

"I think it would be great if you shared what you observed. Would that be okay?" I asked, sensing Dr. Jones's hesitation.

"I noticed that most of them were participating, which was great. I felt disappointed about two team members, if I were to tell you my real feelings. Kathy showed up 45 minutes late with a coffee and no apology. She just strolled in. Tina didn't show up at all. When I asked her about it later, she made some excuse about her office manager not informing her. We had sent many emails and updates. She didn't want to take responsibility."

I stayed silent. I had a sense that Dr. Jones rarely admitted to feelings of anger and frustration—so much so that he would do anything to prevent conflict, even healthy conflict, among his staff. By getting involved in their disagreements, Dr. Jones was reinforcing the character roles of the drama triangle.[24] This is a common dynamic in the workplace as well as in other types of interpersonal and family interactions.

The drama triangle includes three character roles: a rescuer, a persecutor and a victim. In Dr. Jones's offices, the office staff were playing the victim role. When they were held accountable by the managers (the villains, or persecutors in this triangle) the staff would complain to Dr. Jones, who, instead of coaching and authorizing the office managers to handle the situation, would swoop in to be the hero and rescuer.—The classic drama triangle.

When these dynamics arise, people may recognize that they are playing any one of these three roles, none of which are healthy or empowered.

....

24. Stephen Karpman MD, "Fairy Tales and Script Drama Analysis," *Transactional Analysis Bulletin* 26, no. 7 (1968): 39-43

Once you recognize what's going on, you can extract yourself from the drama triangle.[25]

I shared the concept of the drama triangle with Dr. Jones and asked him what he made of it. "I understand the idea and I see how you are placing each of the people," he said. "The office staff feel upset and can feel like victims. Yes, of course, when there is a victim, there has to be a bad guy. And to be honest, I feel that it is my role to guide and serve my employees. If that means I'm a hero or rescuer, I'm okay with that."

"I think you get a lot of esteem and confidence in helping others. I think a part of what makes you successful is that you are an advocate for employees and family members."

"Yes, exactly! Helping others, starting with being the eldest of four, is what I've always done."

"Perhaps we can explore what it means to be an advocate versus what it means to be a hero. What are your thoughts?"

"An advocate is on your side and wants to see you succeed. And a hero ... well, going back to what you said before, maybe a hero is someone who wants to rescue. From having two children of my own and many nieces and nephews, I know that when you want someone to learn something, you should guide them and not do it for them. ... Okay, I'm starting to see what you mean."

"You shared that you want your team to be self-sufficient, that you don't want to always intervene. Perhaps there are times when you can be an advocate and times when you can be a hero?"

"Perhaps I can role practice with the staff on how to approach and respond to the office managers. At the same time, I can work with the office managers to soften their style."

"That sounds like a good plan. You'll be helping all of them to learn a new way to communicate. What happens along the way when a staff member calls you?"

....

25.   David Emerald, *The Power of TED,* 3rd ed. (Polaris Publishing, 2016), 1-138.

"Good question. I will coach each person instead of coming down to the office and making it a whole production. I don't have the time and it's not empowering to them. It will also be less emotionally exhausting for me! Being a hero is too much work. I'll work on being an advocate!" he exclaimed.

Over the ensuing months, I worked with Dr. Jones to role practice the coaching conversations he wanted to have with his office managers. He infused his warm style into the conversations and made sure he and the office managers followed up with each person. I also worked with each office manager to develop a warm and constructive style. Two low performers left within that time.

Dr. Jones and I also talked about the roots of where he'd learned to avoid conflict. He shared that he rarely saw his parents arguing and conflicts made him uncomfortable. As we worked together, he reported feeling better equipped to drive his own powerful conversations with office managers, vendors and partners. He confessed to slipping once when he went into the office and heard a staff member complaining, but then realized he was falling into the hero role and went back to coaching her.

After several months of coaching, I collaborated with Dr. Jones on creating a more open workplace environment through group coaching. The early sessions had tension, suspicion, side glances and folded arms. Dr. Jones was transparent in what he wanted for the group. "I want to keep a nice culture and at the same time, create a space to speak the truth. The managers are going to coach their teams and hold them accountable. I will no longer get involved in your office challenges. I trust you to handle them."

Through helping Dr. Jones and the office managers develop coaching skills, the office evolved toward an environment that was more open and honest. Over time, the office managers became more comfortable bringing up tough issues. Months later, Dr. Jones told me he felt so much more relaxed and appreciated that he could name what had been happening using the seagull syndrome and the drama triangle concepts. "I can identify now when I'm being pulled in, and guess what? Not my job!" he said proudly.

SUMMARY

If you possess an indirect style, you relate well to others like you. Considerate, gentle with feedback and frequently checking in to see how people feel, your style brings harmony and comfort. In the best-case scenario, you will create alignment and build loyalty for your people-centered style—if you also initiate honest conversations and hold people accountable for their performance. In the worst-case scenario, you will avoid conflict by brushing issues under the rug and telling yourself, "It's not that important," or, "I don't want to hurt his feelings," leading to a culture of false harmony. This environment may look good on the outside, but unsaid things remain brewing under the surface.

Leadership style
Indirect, avoids confrontation, hyperaware of other people's feelings.

Result
A "nice" and comfortable environment where conflict is seen as something negative that employees should avoid.

Impact
People avoid speaking the truth to fit in with culture. Important discussions about raising performance are neglected. People may not know the direction of the organization and feel fearful to inquire. Low performers remain on the staff even though they bring down the rest of the team's performance. Straightforward types look like jerks if they don't modify their style.

Realization
Create an environment where open communication exists and uncovers conflict.

Examine Your Blueprint
Explore your mindset on your own and then with a trusted colleague or coach. Consider the origins of your leadership style and new ways of looking at it.

🗣 Examine Your Blueprint

Growing up, what messages did I receive about not speaking up? Where did these messages come from, what were the influencing factors (e.g., family dynamics, culture, gender, class, etc.)?

Where did not speaking up help me?

Where does my not speaking up currently hurt me?

What message does my style send to my colleagues?

What might creating more accountability look like?

What behaviors should I change so that I can role-model what I want from others?

ACTION STEPS

- Think about a person who has a more direct style that appeals to you. If possible, observe how they initiate powerful conversations. Ask this person to coach you through getting ready to initiate a conversation you need to have.
- Envision a future where you authentically express yourself with ease, directly and respectfully. How are you feeling? What do your relationships look like? Consider how avoiding conflict is a disservice to you and the other person and how it may also keep you from being who you want to be.
- Observe your feelings and the outcomes they produce when you avoid conflict by silently keeping things in, sharing a message that is full of fillers, or speaking passive-aggressively (remember the key word in passive aggressive is aggressive).
- Practice being less attached to outcomes so that when people or events you invest in don't turn out as you expect, you can take it less personally. This will help you be self-expressed without being paralyzed that someone may get mad at you.
- Fight your fears of speaking up by learning simple communication models like Situation-Behavior-Impact (SBI)[26] where you share the situation as if it were recorded (what happened, when and with whom), the behavior and the impact it had on you and others.

----

26. Situation-Behavior-Impact is a communication model developed by the Center for Creative Leadership (https://www.ccl.org/) to drive important conversations and share feedback and observations.

Analysis Paralysis Is Real:
Listen Up, Loosen Up and Take a Leap

A leader who is detail-oriented and talented at executing a project from inception to implementation is a key asset to any organization, particularly when the leader is collaborative and accepting of change. However, the strength of this type of leader can also become their weakness when they get trapped in the details and have a hard time seeing the big picture, causing them to resist change and innovation. Innovating requires different approaches, including freeing up your time from meetings, carving out time to think and create, networking internally and externally and challenging your automatic thinking so you view things as possibilities.

Hui Yin was a manager at a furniture manufacturing company and a candidate for a promotion to a director role. I found her professional and well-prepared in our first phone call, albeit slightly skeptical about executive coaching. She shared that she had received positive feedback from her boss and the CEO and was not sure what she would gain from our working together. "I've got my teams in order and my processes in place finally—only now I'm being told that I need to innovate. I don't know what they mean by that. I've done my job well and have received positive performance reviews. But I'm hearing that I need to think bigger if I want to get to the next level here. I admit that I'm perplexed and frustrated about what they want from me." After talking about how coaching would be a safe space to discuss these challenges and look for growth opportunities, Hui Yin seemed to loosen up a bit. I assured her that her feedback would be held in confidence and we would be sharing only her goals with her supervisor.

Entering the conference room ten minutes before our meeting to set up, I was surprised to see Hui Yin seated at the end of the table, all settled in. She had dark shoulder-length thick hair and was wearing a light blue poplin shirt. She had a steaming cup of coffee and bottle of water to the left and a small tablet and several pens and highlighters to the right. In front of her was a yellow notebook propped up by a metal book stand. This was a woman with a plan. I liked her already.

"Good morning, Doc!" she said with a smile.

"Hi, Hui Yin, great to meet you in person. You look like you're ready to go!"

"Yes, I was born ready," she chuckled, a twinkle in her eyes.

I believed her. I had heard a lot of positive feedback about how organized and detail-oriented Hui Yin was, staying ahead of deadlines and making sure her team did the same. I had spoken with ten of her colleagues in preparation for creating the feedback report and learned that Hui Yin was excellent at taking a project from inception to delivery. The challenge the VP and CEO had was that when it came to proposed changes to methods, systems, or processes, Hui Yin tended to get critical in the moment, firing off one question after another and sharing many reasons for why the change could fail. This was becoming exhausting for the cross-functional teams she worked with. The VP and CEO also wanted Hui Yin to start coming up with and driving innovation. They shared with me that Hui Yin's excellent execution skills were no longer enough. For her to reach the next level of director and to help the company grow, she had to develop a more open style to help drive change and innovation. When I asked the CEO what would happen if Hui Yin did not make this leap, I saw his smile turning into a straight line. "Hui Yin will stagnate. She'll either rise to this challenge or stay in the same position indefinitely."

Leaning forward, Hui Yin said to me, "I did all my prep work and I'm assuming you did yours. I'm ready to review the feedback."

We discussed the 360-degree input on Hui Yin's strengths of connecting well with others, being a great coach, having the skill set to take projects to completion and being detail-oriented and committed. Then we moved on to the areas for improvement:

> "Hui Yin likes to work on things that she gets immediate positive feedback for. I see room for progress in Hui Yin thinking more strategically, for the long term at a high level and putting more time into getting the group to create a structure so she is out of the weeds more."

> "She has a hard time moving the ball and can get 'analysis paralysis.'"

> "She doesn't want to try new things."

"It's so common to hear her say, 'We tried that before,' or, 'That will never work.'"

"She's not strategic; she's tactical."

"What do you think, Hui Yin?"

"Well, I thought I was being strategic, but maybe I have a different definition from other people," she trailed off, as she stared out the window at the tall weeping willow tree dancing in the wind. From the third-floor window, we could see people coming into work.

"Those people," she said, "depend on me to be there for them and help them. What happens to my coaching them if I'm off innovating?" She leaned forward and seemed somewhat perturbed.

"You received some positive feedback about your coaching style and how you support your team. That's something to celebrate. Let's not take that for granted. You told me it's part of why you're being considered for promotion to director. The question is: What do you think should be next for you?"

"Wow, you're good! Making me feel proud of myself for a minute, remembering what I told you!" she said with a chuckle and sat down again. "Okay, so I do say those things about having tried some of those things before. I've been in this business for almost twenty years now. I do have experience."

"I hear that. I'm wondering if your colleagues have wisdom you can tap into."

"My team members do bring forward some good ideas. It takes more time to meet for that, of course. Perhaps it could help if I stretch more."

"What can be a first step?"

"Well, maybe I can stop sounding like a Negative Nell. I've observed the body language of people when I do that and they seem to shut down."

"Nice observation. What else have you considered?"

"I need to have time to think. The way things are now, I have back-to-back meetings and my people are always seeking feedback from me."

We discussed further how Hui Yin spent her time and came up with a series of actions that would help her make some modifications. They included declining certain meetings and instead having team members attend and report back; making "thinking appointments" with herself, putting a do not disturb sign on the door; and seeking input from "innovative and dreamer type" team members and the down-to-earth staff alike.

Over the next four months, Hui Yin worked on several things. One focus was being centered during meetings. She noticed that her head would spin when meeting with the creative dreamer types. "They fire off one idea after the next. I can barely keep up with them. I just breathe like we talked about, stay centered and ask questions calmly. It hasn't been easy, but I think I'm making progress."

Hui Yin also started attending industry networking events, even though she hated them in the beginning. "Doc, there were so many people in the room, it was a bit overwhelming." She changed her vocabulary when meeting with managers of other divisions. Her response went from, "We've tried that before," to, "Tell me more." She was particularly proud of this shift. In our conversations, she would frequently joke around and say, "Tell me more, Doc."

At our next in-person session, Hui Yin shared how hard it was not to attend all the meetings she wanted, although it was saving her time. An area she was particularly proud of, which continued to be challenging, was showing up in a more open way, even when she thought an idea made no sense at all. "This is such a stretch for me. It's not easy, but I'm working on it."

Toward the end of the coaching engagement, I spoke with several of her feedback providers again. They all shared that they had observed a change in Hui Yin's demeanor. She was more open and relaxed and less judgmental of new ideas. The VP shared that it was refreshing to hear Hui Yin come up with new ideas and they were excited to help her develop her leadership potential.

"Who knew I had it in me?" Hui Yin commented as she read her final progress feedback report. "I changed my thinking and started new things. I've turned on a whole new part of myself! And, by the way, my boss told me I'm likely to get the director position next year."

SUMMARY

Companies need detail-oriented leaders who can take projects from inception to completion. Leaders also need to build skills in being creative, strategic and innovative to play a role in their company's growth. It takes time and effort. It may be a stretch to collaborate with innovators and others who see the world differently from you. It may be uncomfortable to attend events and be the one to present your thoughts. These very challenges can also be an amazing way for you to expand your abilities and viewpoints.

Leadership Style
Detailed, focused, talented at execution, questions new ideas for better and worse.

Result
Can shut people down; employees stop sharing ideas.

Impact
Contributes to stagnation and not introducing new products or services to customers.

Realization
Make space for coming up with new ideas; update understanding of innovation; be open to seeking, receiving and exploring fresh insights.

Examine Your Blueprint
Explore your mindset on your own and then with a trusted colleague or coach. Consider the origins of your leadership style and new ways of looking at it.

Examine Your Blueprint

Where did I learn this style of work?

How is it helping me?

Where is this preventing success?

Whom have I observed with a style that is detailed and creative?

How can focusing on innovation help me, my team and my company grow?

ACTION STEPS

- Start your own networking group with like-minded people in your industry.
- Read trade and industry journals.
- Keep up on business trends through relevant news outlets.
- Get to know different aspects of your organization. Have lunch or coffee with the heads of different departments and learn how all the parts work together.
- During brainstorm sessions or when people share ideas, control the urge to say things like, "We tried that before," or, "I'm not sure that's a good idea." Be mindful of your body language as well.
- Seek ideas from different generations in your workplace.
- Work with a facilitator who can bring out the ideas of your team, allowing you to participate.
- Interview the biggest dreamers you know. Take notes. Nod. Say thank you. Review your notes and look for themes. Come up with possible solutions. Go back and get input from the dreamers.

SAFETY VERSUS RISK

Idea Overload with Not-So-Great Execution:
Stop Throwing Spaghetti and Sit Down and Listen

A leader who is big-picture oriented and talented at bringing new ideas to the organization has the typical entrepreneur persona. Fast-thinking and in constant motion, these leaders are always three steps ahead and examine every piece of information through the lens of innovation. The strengths of this type of leader can become overplayed, causing them to regularly bring in new ideas and methodologies that create more waves than people can handle and lead to difficulty in understanding, prioritizing, or executing direction. Sticking with the plan and balancing innovation—rather than bringing on a new "flavor of the week" to-do list—requires building new habits, such as seeking input from others, determining priorities and seeing these through. It also includes sharing the vision and purpose regularly and creating space for the implementing types, who tend to be awesome at executing the plan and risk-averse to sharing concerns.

Ben entered the room like a gust of wind. "Hi, Shahrzad. How's it going?" he greeted me with his left hand as he balanced a thick stack of folders in the crook of his right arm. He closed the door slowly and sat down. Tall, tan, lean and in his early forties, I detected a bit of nervous energy beneath Ben's mostly calm demeanor. He was the CEO of his own surf wear company and anxious to keep growing the organization but was facing some pushback from his team.

"I'm working on being more centered and focused, but I think it will take me a while. My best peace is on my surfboard or just hanging with my kids and wife."

"No doubt," I responded with a smile, appreciating his positive energy. The conference room reflected Ben's passions with the largest glass window facing the Pacific Ocean. I glanced around the spacious room and noted the white boardroom table and crisp white leather chairs. On the far left of the room were eight flipchart papers with diagrams and sketches. A large white surfboard with orange accents hung horizontally on the wall opposite the grand ocean view window. Ben had brought his Zen into this meeting space.

In our pre-meeting call, Ben shared that he wanted to make sure his company culture was on track and that his people would be open to the many changes he had planned. After seven years of success in surf gear, he had expanded into casual clothing for men and women. "We're on a roll, but we'll stagnate and fall behind the competition if we stop innovating." However, Ben was facing some resistance from his staff. When he shared new ideas or sought feedback, he either experienced silence or reluctant responses. "Half of the group nods and agrees with my ideas; the other half tells me why the new direction won't work. I don't feel good about making demands and having a patriarchal culture where the vibe is, 'Do what I say, or you'll get fired.' I hired a smart team and I want them to share their ideas and concerns."

I had solicited feedback from Ben's team on his management style. "I'm looking forward to hearing my team's comments. I'll see it as a gift, as you suggested!" he said with a smile. I noticed a slight tap of his right foot under the table. I could only guess that Ben had boundless energy throughout each day.

As we read through the feedback, words like "bright, unflappable, creative genius and passionate" were some of the descriptions that people had shared about Ben.

"Let's get into the other stuff," he exclaimed as he peeled off his brightly striped hoodie. As I expected, he was ready to go. But he sat still, breathing deeply, as we went through the feedback on the areas for development.

> "I appreciate how creative Ben is, but he can overwhelm us with ideas. I don't know how to respond sometimes."

> "I wonder if Ben could talk about his new ideas in a way that shows he has thought about the potential pros and cons. Some of us feel silly asking the detailed questions, because we don't want to come across as if we don't believe in his ideas. When we ask questions, he seems to get offended or says we are being 'dream killers.'"

> "We are sometimes given tasks before we know the bigger purpose of the project."

"Sometimes Ben will start several new initiatives at once. We don't know where to focus or prioritize."

Ben asked, "Do you mind if I take a moment to process this? I'd like to sit on my mat and play a meditation on my phone. You can join me. Is that okay?"

"Sure," I said, glad I had worn loose pants and flats on this particular day. How cool is it that he realizes he needs a moment? I thought. He pulled out two cushions and we moved toward the window and sat down.

After five minutes, Ben said he was ready to go back to work. We settled into the white leather chairs. "How is the feedback resonating with you?"

"Look, there will always be employees who want to slow down and get more facts. But in the start-up world, you need to move quickly. We don't have the luxury of creating every plan perfectly. This is part of my frustration."

"I understand where you're coming from. You need to stay agile and inno-vative. Excelling at execution is a strength in a start-up. I wonder how your dynamic might shift if more of the team had *your* style."

"My team brings me back to reality. I'll admit that it feels like they hold me back at times, but they've definitely saved me plenty with their detailed questions."

We sat silently for a moment. Ben spoke first. "I do get mad at their reac-tions sometimes. I guess it comes from my past."

"Tell me more about that."

"My dad was an engineer who tried to be an entrepreneur. He had one failed idea after another. I felt so bad for him. I remember the tension when my parents fought about money, wanting my dad to succeed in his ventures and wishing my mom would give him a chance. I wanted him to say, 'At least I'm trying something new!' I relate the questions of my staff to when my mom would question my dad's ideas. I remember thinking that she could have been more supportive."

"I can see how this dynamic could bring up negative experiences from the past. If we could shift gears for a moment, what do you think are the best and worst qualities of entrepreneurs?"

"We love new ideas and everything feels possible. My mind is always scanning for opportunities. My wife Janna says I was born with this instinct. Okay, now you're probably waiting for when the strength turns into a weakness, right? I remember you talking about something like that in our first call."

Smiling, I gestured for him to continue.

"I see a possibility and I get excited. I rush to the office and want to share it with Elizabeth, my CFO."

"How does that typically go?"

"I see this disapproving look on her face and it kills me! My mom would give my dad that look. I hate it! I sometimes tell Elizabeth, 'Stop being a dream killer! I'm trying to grow this company!'"

"What do you think your reaction is telling you?"

"That part of me still carries some baggage from my childhood. I've read about the amygdala hijack and how we lose our sh——t when we get triggered by an old memory. Damn!"

"What do you think Elizabeth is seeking?"

"She wants to make sure we keep the company on track and I'm coming in with ideas that may seem crazy to her; then I get mad, which helps nothing. Honestly, she is doing her job as CFO! I don't want her colluding with every crazy idea I have. She is here to protect us and create a balance."

He paused and looked out at the ocean, "I think we're getting somewhere." I nodded and stayed still. "I can change this!" He turned his gaze back to me.

"What can be a first step?"

"I have all these great minds in the office. I can vet my ideas first."

We brainstormed other steps, such as getting input so his ideas would have the right amount of detail before he presented them to others; and seeking help from his executive team in prioritizing his innovations to focus on one thing at a time. Ben agreed that it would be helpful to reframe his dream killer term to "company keeper," which incorporated the positive aspects of his team's behavior instead of focusing on how the behavior made him feel.

Several months later, Elizabeth shared with me that Ben seemed less anxious. "He applies his mindfulness practice to how he introduces ideas to the company. It's calmer and more well-thought-out. He's also open to hearing my ideas now. What did you do to Ben?"

I smiled and said, "It was in him. He just had to discover it for himself."

SUMMARY

The best part of the innovating style is having an entrepreneurial spirit and creating new ways to make the most of any situation. This type of leader brings in excitement, fresh ideas and new ways of looking at work and the world; they see possibilities for untapped potential everywhere. But this style becomes overplayed when too many ideas are presented and started one after another, without clear communication. If you are this leader, you can benefit from seeking input, prioritizing new initiatives, breaking down projects into manageable tasks and using discipline to stick with existing projects instead of neglecting them for a new idea.

Leadership Style
Creative, exciting, works in bursts of energy, believes in possibility and that most ideas should be implemented.

Result
Too many ideas introduced simultaneously causing strain, confusion and change fatigue.

Impact

When innovation is in excess, many things are started and few things are taken to completion. When this style is balanced with openness to feedback from detail-oriented types and those executing on the ground, there can be a marriage of the big picture and details, reviewing risk and taking risk, ultimately helping the company thrive.

Realization

Vetting, pacing and prioritizing innovation drives success. Ensure that your team has a balance of styles to bring out the best in the company and that the strengths of the dreamers and those executing change are recognized and harmonized.

Examine Your Blueprint

Explore your mindset on your own and then with a trusted colleague or coach. Consider the origins of your leadership style and new ways of looking at it.

Examine Your Blueprint

Where did I learn my creative style of work?

How is it helping me?

Where is this preventing success?

Whom have I observed with a style that's creative and structured for implementation?

How can focusing on how I see and introduce innovation help me, my team and my company grow?

ACTION STEPS

- Vet your ideas with two or three people you consider detailed types.
- Find your inner patient person as the detailed types tell you the reasons your idea may not work.
- When introducing a new idea, seek input on the timing.
- Scale your skill by having workshops on what you do to find new ideas. Teach your team how you scan your environment to learn about current challenges and potential opportunities.

 TODAY VERSUS TOMORROW

No More Firefighting:
Get Focused, Create Direction and Get Started

If creating systems, structures and processes is the strength of the organized type, then responding to emergencies with ease, meeting issues in the moment and even flourishing in chaos are the strengths of the flexible type of leader. This leader will likely be a great partner in a start-up setting or any environment with rapidly changing needs or a quickly evolving culture (e.g., post-merger, serving in emergencies, etc.). This way of leading has multiple advantages: few freaking-out moments when issues emerge; problems are addressed quickly; and order is restored in a timely manner. These leaders thrive when problem-solving under pressure and often come out as the hero.

But this style can become a liability if hero syndrome sets in and everything is handled in this extremely responsive manner. This person gets such physical and emotional energy from responding to challenges that they tend to play the hero and provide answers right away, rather than taking the time to train others to find their own answers. The leader may gravitate toward managing tasks that aren't urgent versus attending to longer-term tasks that require focus, detail and attention. When a flexible style of leadership is imbalanced, people will stagnate and the organization will not reach its strategic goals. The leader will be too busy firefighting and solving everyone's problems, looking to be a hero.

Self-Check: Hero Syndrome

- Do you have an extreme desire to be needed, appreciated and valued?
- Do you overextend yourself to help others?
- Do you find it difficult to say no to colleagues?
- Does the thought of laying down boundaries make you cringe?
- Do you find yourself favoring "firefighting" over engaging in more strategic endeavors and long-term work/planning?

Drew had risen quickly through the ranks of a multinational food processing plant, growing from manager to director within five years. He had a bounce in his step as he walked into the company's slightly dated conference room. He was a fit, medium-built man with green eyes and salt-and-pepper hair. He had a big smile on his face and seemed excited to start our coaching.

From the 360-degree feedback I'd reviewed, Drew was more of a firefighter than a strategic thinker. "He loves solving problems!" his supervisor wrote. "He's good at it and it's part of what we need. But he needs to figure out how to protect his time and work on strategy. He can 'let go' of some of the tasks he is good at so others can develop. This will be imperative to his growth opportunities."

As we turned through the pages of the report, Drew was pleased to read the many positive comments about his open-door policy and agile style as well as his capacity to handle emergencies well and thrive under pressure. When we made it to the areas for development, I had a feeling that some of the behaviors noted were strengths that had become weaknesses through overuse.

> "Drew handles day-to-day fires well and is quick to solve our problems. Even though this is helpful to us, it would be even more helpful if he taught us to fish and problem-solve on our own."

> "I'm not sure how strategic Drew can be when he is always on call to his team. This helpful behavior seems great on the surface, but in reality, he is not working on the five areas of our strategic plan."

> "It would be helpful if he delegated to us so we could grow and he could do bigger-picture things."

"I wish Drew would let us learn, so we don't have to keep going to him."

Drew and I looked at each other. His expression was neutral. He stretched out his long legs and arms in his ergonomic office chair. Impressed by his ability to take a moment to reflect, I remained still, knowing that this could be a game-changing conversation.

He finally took a deep breath, exhaled slowly and then started speaking. "Look, I have worked hard to help and protect my team from errors. I have an open-door policy and they can come to me for anything. We always make our deadlines and our customers are happy with us. What's the problem really? Isn't this nitpicking?"

I understood where Drew was coming from. Based on the positive feedback, I could see that there were many ways that his behavior and style were a benefit. People said he was helpful, engaging, motivating and a great coach.

"Good questions. Tell me more about what you are thinking."

Drew leaned his elbows on the table. "I see that they care about me and value me. However, I do feel slightly offended that they don't see me as strategic."

"What do you think about the recently updated five areas of the strategic plan that you shared with me in our first meeting?"

Rolling his eyes, he asked, "When would I work on that? Our company has so many last-minute problems and my people always need my help. They love it when I help them."

"And how do you feel when you are helping them?"

"I love it! I can handle their problems quickly and we save a lot of time. I save the day!"

"Like a hero?"

We chuckled and I asked him if he'd heard of the "hero syndrome."[27] He was not clear on it, so I explained: A person with hero syndrome has an unconscious need to be needed, appreciated and valued. On its own, this is something all humans need and want. But in hero syndrome, this need drives the individual to go above and beyond for others to the point where they may neglect their own priorities—which, in Drew's case, was to work the company's strategic plan. Responding to and handling issues gives heroes an energy boost. They know the answers and they want to help. Creating and following a strategic plan seems like such a drag compared to the rush of being a hero. Being on call and helping people with their problems can be highly gratifying.

Drew said it was an interesting concept, but he needed more convincing. "Can I suspend judgment for now?" I appreciated his honesty and shared that perhaps the need to feel appreciated combined with having a flexible leadership style made firefighting more appealing than sticking to a plan. I referred to some data in his feedback report: "Drew will just tell me what to do without trying to coach me. Or he will drive over the next day and handle the issue himself."

Self-check: Firefighting at Work

You may be firefighting instead of strategizing if:

- There's never enough time to solve your problems.
- Solutions are incomplete.
- The same problems keep popping up.
- Urgency trumps importance.
- Problems become crises.
- Performance drops.

When I explored this with Drew, he said that his team would not do the job as well and would likely make errors. "What would happen if you taught your number two and number three people some critical skills for handling emergencies?" I inquired.

"I would have some more time on my hands, that's for sure."

....

27. Laura Berman Fortgang, "Getting Off-Course: The Hero Syndrome," HuffPost, updated November 23, 2012, https://www.huffpost.com/entry/hero-syndrome_b_1900657.

"I'm wondering if being a hero might be holding you back from other things?"

"Yes, I'm seeing it. Okay, let's make a plan!"

Drew agreed to work on two things. The first was to read a *Harvard Business Review* (HBR) article on the symptoms of firefighting at work.[28] Drew said it was as if the article were written for him since he had most of the symptoms. "Sheesh, Doc, I get it! I have incomplete solutions. I rarely create the new systems I need because I'm focused on immediate problem-solving. And I'm losing opportunities to streamline and improve systems, which impacts performance and hurts sales."

The second step was to create and follow five specific steps for going from hero to strategist and redirecting his energies when he wanted to jump in and save the day:

1. Listen and don't react. Take a moment to breathe and reflect.
2. Fight the urge to step in. Read a book of quotes; doodle; journal.
3. Ask coaching questions to guide the person to handle the situation on their own.
4. Go back to working on the company strategy.
5. Have an accountability partner to keep me on track.

A few weeks later, Drew told me he had shared his five steps with his team. They were more than happy to be coached through their challenges and appreciated his humility to change his behavior and help them all grow. He had a couple of slip-ups but was able to get back on track when his colleagues asked, "Shouldn't you be coaching us right now so you reduce your firefighting?"

Several months on, after having empowered his number two and number three people to handle emergencies, Drew said he was growing out of his "superhero phase." He had taken time to streamline processes with input from his team, resulting in fewer repeated challenges. He had received positive feedback on his progress toward the company's strategic goals and enjoyed being held accountable by one of his peers, an organized woman

....

28. Roger Bohn, "Stop Fighting Fires," *Harvard Business Review,* From the Magazine (July–August 2000), https://hbr.org/2000/07/stop-fighting-fires.

who was happy to redirect him when she observed or heard that he was regressing back into his firefighting ways.

SUMMARY

A firefighting style is one where you thrive on solving everyone's problems. Rather than coaching and guiding a team member to think through a decision and make a choice, you effectively tell them the answer and then proceed to complete the task yourself. You believe this saves time. In reality, it keeps others from growing and being empowered to make their own decisions. It may also keep you from working on more important strategic initiatives.

Leadership Style
Agile, problem-solving, moving quickly from one problem to another.

Result
Challenges are handled promptly and emergencies prevented at the expense of working on important strategic initiatives.

Impact
Your people are not trained and empowered to handle things themselves; you don't focus on more important work. You are busy firefighting versus strategically creating new opportunities for the organization.

Realization
You, your team and the company will grow when you empower others. Stop being a hero and dive into the most strategic work.

Examine Your Blueprint
Explore your mindset on your own and then with a trusted colleague or coach. Consider the origins of your leadership style and new ways of looking at it.

Examine Your Blueprint

Where did I learn this style of work?

_____

_____

_____

How is it helping me?

_____

_____

_____

Where is this preventing success?

_____

_____

_____

Whom have I observed with a style that is flexible and focused?

_____

_____

_____

ACTION STEPS

- Regularly refer to and drive toward your company's strategic plan.
- Start developing your number two and number three people by creating a coaching plan and empowering them to make decisions on their own, without always checking with you. Start small and slowly allow the team member to handle bigger decisions.
- Check in regularly with your direct reports' development plan.
- Be okay with teaching skills to your people that could take you out of the equation. Know that this is the only way any of you will grow.

TODAY VERSUS TOMORROW

Perfect Plan May Change:
Get Curious and Agile

When it comes to how leaders achieve goals, at one end of the spectrum are the flexible types: jugglers, multitaskers and firefighters who save the day—but at the expense of strategizing and improving processes that prevent the fires in the first place. At the other end of this spectrum are the structured types: the people who are the first to create tasks, timelines and accountabilities when there is a new project. They are masters at making sure there is clarity on what's expected and by whom; they find comfort in structure. They're proud of the quality of their work, because they spend so much time on perfecting it.

Yes, many structured leaders are perfectionists, which comes with pluses (high-quality beautiful work) and minuses (spending an inordinate amount of time taking something from 95 percent to 98 percent quality). When this strength becomes overplayed, it impacts the leader's ability to respond to incoming information that may potentially change the direction of the project. The structured leader's challenge is to prepare as much as possible *and* stay flexible, open and curious about what may emerge that may create a need for change. No more avoiding new information!

Kayla was a senior manager at a professional services firm. After almost fifteen years in marketing for fast-growth companies, she had met the officers of her current organization when they worked on a project together. They'd offered Kayla a management position after seeing her talent, drive and organized style and she'd gone for it. Working with a Fortune 500 company was a bit of a relief, she said; many of the fast-growth companies she'd worked for experienced a lot of instability due to day-to-day changes.

Even so, her supervisor Jill mentioned that Kayla's need for perfection was creating too much lag time. Kayla would also become frustrated with people's response times and errors. She was also reluctant to pay attention to new information that could alter her "perfect plans." "Kayla's work is flawless," Jill said, "but she is too critical and that holds things up. It's not going to work for us, if this continues."

Kayla and I met in her office. She leaned back on the blue denim couch, carefully adjusting her charcoal shift dress and crossing her tan legs. She tapped her red-bottomed heels up and down. She was so put together and coordinated from head to toe. That also takes thinking and planning. "You seem ready. Shall we dig in?"

"Okay, Doc, let's see what the feedback is. I have a feeling it will say I'm too much of a perfectionist—which I actually like about myself. Sorry not sorry!" she said with a flair of her hand, flashing chunky gold rings and a fresh light pink manicure.

As we moved through the strengths in the report, she recognized that her organized style was responsible for much of her success. "I like how people see that being methodical and sticking with schedules and time-lines is important. I work my rear off to run my projects with precision and perfection!" She made a triangle using her index fingers and thumbs and repeated the movement a couple of times, as if to emphasize what it looked like when things come together.

There were comments about Kayla's work ethic and high standards as well as how she handled problems: "She doesn't romance problems; she solves them," one person wrote. The areas for development seemed to show where her style had become overplayed.

> "Kayla moves quickly with the project and strategy. There are times when it would help to slow down and think bigger picture. Once she is going, she doesn't want anything to get in the way and stop her, so then she is less likely to be open to incoming input. She doesn't take time to stand back and assess if the process is still correct, or ask, 'Are there other variables that need to be considered? Does this way still make sense?'"

> "Rather than seeing new information as messing up your plan, know it will help you later."

> "She has almost constrained herself to thinking just about time and the efficiency of the project rather than also factoring in the impact not paying attention to new information could have on a project."

> "She is so efficient and organized that this can sometimes show up as intolerant to other points of view."

Kayla leaned back, took a sip of water and stared at me.

"How does this resonate with you?" I asked, leaning forward.

"I don't like it, but it's kind of true. After all that hard work of creating a great plan, I get so bothered when it gets changed. I ask myself, 'Why is this necessary?'"

"Tell me more."

"I get so much input from everyone in the beginning. I ask people to share their thoughts. I go back and forth with the client. Everyone sees everything along the way. My scheduling takes into account how we get from here to there as well as people's schedules and challenges. Not to brag, but the final schedule and project plan feels like a work of art. I love creating something that everyone has contributed to and I love following the plan."

"It sounds like your leadership style works well when things stay on plan. What types of situations make the team deviate from the plan?"

"When they hear something worrisome from the client, when they get new information, when some pieces no longer make sense," she said with a sigh. She twirled her hair around her forefinger. Her hair was a perfect ombre— light brown fading into a butter blonde. It was clear that she put a lot of time and thought into whatever she chose to pursue.

"Interesting."

"I've always gotten strong positive feedback about my style. I had a nagging feeling there were downsides, though. It sounds like people want me to be more flexible. But how? It's not my nature! I'm not someone spontaneous who can pick up and go and just change quickly. My husband is one of those people. I appreciate people with that ability. But I'm not one of them!"

"Thanks for talking through this. It definitely is a personality type with its own pros and cons, just like every other personality. This is more about trying a few new techniques versus changing who you are. I'm curious about your energy toward exploring this."

"I have good energy for this. It's a relief to know I don't have to overhaul who I am! Okay, here are a couple of thoughts. Maybe I don't respond right away with an angry email when I get the news that something needs to change."

"What might you do instead?"

"I can take a walk, a few deep breaths—anything but respond!"

"Great. What else comes to mind?

"I can ask more questions. I shouldn't avoid reality. I guess I can re-create the plan given the new information."

I helped Kayla come up with a list of nonthreatening questions she could ask to seek more information. We made sure to avoid starters like, "Why?" and, "How come?" which can be perceived as blaming questions. We talked about taking a relaxed tone and modifying her style, not losing it. She had worked hard to get where she was and was becoming clear on what behaviors she could adapt to continue her trajectory. "I want to be one of those cool, calm leaders with presence, who doesn't get easily rattled. At the same time, I want to be authentic and share my voice as a strong female leader. I can't be afraid of sharing my emotions, whether joy, excitement, disappointment, or anger. We need humanness in the workplace."

I checked in with Kayla throughout the six months of our engagement. She shared that working on her responses, becoming more centered and using coaching questions had given her a greater sense of ease. There were some starts and stops as she developed these new muscles. She did not give up and the feedback reflected this.

> "Kayla seems so much more relaxed now. We're not afraid to share changes or new ideas with her."

> "Now Kayla checks in to see if there are any changes; before, it seemed like she was avoiding me when she knew there could be changes."

As we sat on that same couch, Kayla was all smiles. "I worked hard on this! I put reminders in my calendar and I tracked every time I responded differently."

"Of course, you did!" I exclaimed, high-fiving her.

"Honestly, this has helped me in my personal life as well. I used to get defensive when my husband would change plans. Now I do this thing where I breathe in three times, smile and ask information-seeking questions—like at work. It helps, I tell you! And I'm having more fun."

SUMMARY

The organized leader brings much success to a company. If the person is working in a fast-growth company, there is an ability to make order out of chaos and create systems, structures and processes to help the company become consistent. When a project begins, this person is the first to jump in to organize it from beginning to the end. Creating a path is a natural strength that shows up in all aspects of the person's life—from personal and family needs to the workplace, everything is taken care of on schedule, if not before. But this strength can become a liability if the leader becomes closed to new information. Avoiding emergent information from clients and colleagues can cause missed opportunities. Creating a perfect plan that does not flex is like using a map on your phone that does not redirect you when you make a different turn. It also causes tension with those who need more flexibility in their planning and execution style. By taking small steps to be open to change, a structured leader can make a great impact on the organization.

Leadership Style
Organized, structured, methodical, detailed, ready to start and complete projects.

Result
Deadlines are rarely missed and projects are completed to perfection. Downsides include avoiding conversations around change and missing important incoming information.

Impact
Too much time spent on projects with a focus on perfection, resulting in impatience with others and avoiding facts that may change the plan. This contributes to getting off track and not meeting the strategy.

Realization
Learn how to get centered and be open to new feedback.

Examine Your Blueprint
Explore your mindset on your own and then with a trusted colleague or coach. Consider the origins of your leadership style and new ways of looking at it.

Examine Your Blueprint

Where did I learn this style of work?

_____

_____

_____

How is it helping me?

_____

_____

_____

Where is this preventing success?

_____

_____

_____

Whom have I observed with a style that is flexible and focused?

_____

_____

_____

How can staying open to emerging information help me, my team and my company grow?

_____

_____

_____

ACTION STEPS

- Involve key stakeholders when creating project plans and timelines.
- Know that some people have a completely opposite, emergent style that may offer ways to improve the work.
- Get input as you create timelines and have regular check-in dates to ensure that the project is on track.
- Build structure with room for flexibility.
- Share your best practices with flexible-type leaders.

I wouldn't be surprised if you might see yourself or someone you know or work with in these case studies, as they depict patterns that I've observed over more than two decades of working with clients. It's natural for the behaviors that are our strengths in some areas to present as challenges or even weaknesses in other settings. The first step is awareness of the issue and how it is impacting us; noticing what our leadership style is or patterns we may be in that prevent us from gaining the results we desire.

What opportunities might we be missing because of this behavior? How might this style be hurting your team, culture and organization? What relationships are struggling or in jeopardy because of this behavior? What heights may we fail to reach because of this behavior? I've designed the DRIVE IT model to help you process a professional or personal challenge for yourself or others. The tools at the end of each section support this as well.

Culture Cultivators: Four Keys to Creating a Thriving Culture

Just as it is important to know what to pay attention to and improve in the form of coaching for you or your leaders around the Culture Stressors, it is also important to be aware of positive actions that will help your culture thrive. Culture Cultivators are best practices that will help you grow and manage your culture. The four best practices I've seen among high-performing organizations for cultivating a healthy culture are: (1) develop employee abilities; (2) communicate direction and change; (3) value people: create an environment where diversity, equity and inclusion (DEI) is a way of being; ensure that women, minorities and generations in the workplace are a big part of your workplace and have a sense of belonging; and (4) flex with flexible work. Volumes have been written on these subjects, so following is a snapshot on these four points.

Develop Employee Abilities

Developing employees' skills involves helping them to grow in their capabilities so they can grow in your company. By building employees' skills, you will create a talent pool that meets your company needs while simultaneously engaging your team members. Professional development is deeply valued by employees, particularly millennials.

Target recently decided to pay for tuition for its frontline employees.[29] All U.S. part-time and full-time team members will be eligible for debt-free undergraduate degrees, certificates, certification and free textbooks with no out-

....

29. Target, "Target Launching Debt-Free Education Assistance Program to More Than 340,000 Frontline Team Members," A Bullseye View, Target Corporate, August 4, 2021, https://corporate. target.com/press/releases/2021/08/Target-Launching-Debt-Free-Education-Assistance-Pr.

of-pocket costs as of their first day of work at Target. In addition to Target strengthening its workforce's education and employee loyalty, this bold move will hopefully encourage other companies to follow its lead.

You can measure the return on your investment on training in many ways, including improvements in job performance, customer satisfaction and most importantly, the retention of high performers. The cost of replacing an individual employee can range from half to twice the employee's annual salary. Gallup estimates that a 100-person organization paying an annual average salary of $50,000 per person could have turnover and replacement costs of approximately $660,000 to $2.6 million per year.[30] Aside from cost is the pain of recruiting, interviewing, onboarding and training a new person. This process can be quite lengthy.

Develop your team by creating a learning culture where people have development opportunities through mentors and internal staff as well as through external training and coaching. Training your team members in basic coaching skills can create a coaching culture where giving and receiving coaching is the norm. The more you create a culture of coaching, the easier it will be for people to give feedback to peers and across functions.

Communicate Direction and Change

When I conduct culture assessments, I often see feedback around ambiguity of company vision, direction and goals. Strategy that outlines the company's vision, values and main goals on a single page should be clear to every team member, in every language that is spoken.

Next is the importance of managing change. Change is constant and necessary for an organization to thrive. But employees often resist change for reasons such as lack of transparency and rationale for the change. People are more likely to accept and embrace change when it's managed with planning, clear communication and attention.

In a paragraph, the main steps of change are: Plan the change; get feedback from trusted employees with formal and informal authority across the different levels of the organization; create a written plan that is broken down

....

30. Shane McFeeley and Ben Wigert, "This Fixable Problem Costs U.S. Businesses $1 Trillion," Gallup, March 13, 2019, https://www.gallup.com/workplace/247391/fixable-problem-costs-businesses-trillion.aspx.

into steps, with opportunities to celebrate small wins along the way; communicate regularly; and engage Culture Guardians to support the change and educate others.

Value Your People

Respectful communication and engagement with every level of staff—from frontline crew to executives—and ensuring that managers give employees constructive feedback is part of valuing your team. Valuing your people also means understanding their unique backgrounds and what their diverse perspectives add to the workplace. This includes ensuring that diversity, equity and inclusion are part of your culture.

Diversity is the who: who is recruited and promoted, who is represented and has a seat at the table when it comes to differing and intersecting identities, including those of gender, race, ethnicity, sexual orientation, ability and age. Equity is the what: the opportunities people have access to. Inclusion is the how: how diversity is welcomed and embraced throughout the organization and leadership; how behaviors that galvanize a diversity of voices and identities are demonstrated and encouraged; how people of various groups are encouraged to express themselves and how their presence and perspectives are valued. When you take time to ensure that people are included, you will create a sense of well-being and belonging, feelings that employees cherish and appreciate. Employees who feel that they belong are likely to be more committed to your organization.

Make Diversity, Equity and Inclusion a Way of Being

We all have biases, even if we aren't always aware of them. A bias is an inclination or prejudice we hold, with or without our knowledge, about individuals, groups, or things. It's human nature to categorize information as a way to help us make quick decisions in fight-or-flight situations. We often learn biases from our upbringing, family of origin, community, society and experiences. However, these biases can cause us to discriminate against those who are different from us. Some common biases in the workplace center around identities of gender, social status, race, culture, abilities, age and sexual orientation.

Some of the most important ways to build relationships with your employees are by being aware of your biases and keeping them in check; protecting employees from biases and ensuring you have an inclusive culture where each individual's unique voice is heard and appreciated. If you don't, your people will feel disconnected from you, your mission and your company.

The urgent need for change in incorporating DEI in organizations was expanded following the social justice protests in the summer of 2020. After the world watched George Floyd murdered by a police officer in broad daylight despite the pleas of bystanders, American citizens protested in a way that has never been seen before. Millions of people in the United States had an awakening about the country's roots. Despite the risks of catching the COVID-19 virus, people protested in all fifty states and eventually around the world. Statues of generals and leaders who had supported slavery and colonialism were torn down.

In a new way, people realized something that we'd known all along: the United States, as great a country as it is and as proud of this nation as we are, has a history of slavery. It is sad to say and to write, but the economic infrastructure of the United States prospered because of slavery. This foundation continues to play a large part in the systemic racist undertones and police brutality in the United States. Immigrants and people of color continue to face discrimination in the workplace and in society. Social justice; respect for diversity; and zero tolerance of racist behavior, bias and harassment are more important now than ever.

In the wake of the George Floyd protests, many companies created DEI officer positions and teams to develop diverse, safe and welcoming workplaces that reduce and call out harassment, microaggression and discrimination. The DEI officer ensures that diversity is incorporated into the entire employee experience and that the company operates in a way that is inclusive and welcoming of all employees.

What's good for people is good for business, too. Creating and sustaining a diverse and inclusive workplace leads to multiple benefits: higher revenue growth;[31] increased ability to recruit a more diverse talent pool; and over five

....

31.   Claire Hastwell, "Racially Diverse Workplaces Have Largest Revenue Growth," Great Place to Work, January 4, 2020, https://www.greatplacetowork.com/resources/blog/racially-diverse-workplaces-have-largest-revenue-growth.

times' greater employee retention.[32] Racial and gender diversity are associated with increased sales revenue and greater profits, according to an assessment published in the *American Sociological Review.*[33] McKinsey's research shows that companies in the top quartile for racial and ethnic workplace diversity are 35 percent more likely to have higher returns than their national industry medians.[34]

DEI is not only about who you bring into the organization, who is present at the table (positions with voice and power) and to whom you are listening. It's also about becoming aware of one's own biases and working to uncover unconscious bias. This can include deeply-rooted subconscious biases about race, gender, appearance, age, wealth, etc., that influence and drive decision-making at all levels regarding who is hired, promoted and invested in in the workplace. When leaders engage in DEI training, they gain awareness of bias-related pitfalls and can work to avoid these throughout the talent management process, from recruiting and interviewing to hiring and promoting.

There are several steps to creating a more diverse and inclusive company at the system level and individual level. When you include diverse employees in decision-making, they will come up with unique, different and better ideas than if you had a homogenous group of leaders with similar backgrounds.

Some leaders say that it is difficult to bring on women or people of color for key positions. Consider bringing in someone who can grow into the position. You may hesitate to bring on seemingly less qualified people to expand your diversity, but you won't know the outcome until you take that step. It may take extra effort as well as examining your own unconscious biases; for example, is there some part of you that thinks that certain types of people don't make good leaders?

At the system level, the first step is to review and revamp all processes regarding how people are recruited, how the talent pool is managed and how people are promoted. One way you can observe how much diversity

....

32. Matt Bush, "Why Is Diversity & Inclusion in the Workplace Important?" Great Place to Work, April 13, 2021, https://www.greatplacetowork.com/resources/blog/why-is-diversity-inclusion-in-the-workplace-important.

33. Cedric Herring, "Does Diversity Pay? Race, Gender and the Business Case for Diversity." *American Sociological Review*, April 2009.

34. Sundiatu Dixon-Fyle et al., "Diversity Wins: How Inclusion Matters," McKinsey and Company, May 19, 2020, https://www.mckinsey.com/featured-insights/diversity-and-inclusion/diversity-wins-how-inclusion-matters.

an organization has is to look at the senior team. Are there people of color and women in key positions? Is there a diversity of backgrounds? Examine the makeup of the managers to consider the ratio of men to women and the age brackets of your leaders. Exploring and expanding your organization's diversity will create thriving roots for your organization.

Offering ongoing DEI training that is tied to your values can be a powerful way to message the importance of DEI in your company. It also creates opportunity for staff to learn about the biases we all have and how to reframe them as well as how to handle microaggressions.

You can encourage diversity and inclusion in day-to-day life. This can be done by creating a diversity and inclusion task force to provide input and suggestions. Some very initial steps can include acknowledging staff's various cultural traditions and celebrating holidays of different countries. These small steps bring awareness of other cultures and can be empowering and fun for everyone. When I share Iranian New Year traditions with others, I enjoy it and people walk away learning something new.

Many companies that want to incorporate diversity and inclusion empower employees to form employee resource groups (ERGs), also known as affinity groups, where employees come together based on shared characteristics or life experiences (for example, women, African Americans, Asian Americans, Muslims, LGBTQ+, etc.). These groups, which are sponsored by the company, encourage employees to come together to share their experiences and can also organize group events to provide education for other employees.

At the individual level, it's helpful for managers to learn that not all employees will feel comfortable with certain directions such as, "Just confront him," or, "Take charge and make an executive decision when your boss is not there," or, "You need to talk about your accomplishments publicly." Factors like age, ethnic origin, or if a person is first-generation American can influence whether someone feels comfortable speaking up to their boss, making big decisions on someone else's behalf, or sharing their wins. This has something to do with what Geert Hofstede, an intercultural communication researcher, terms "power distance": "the extent to which the less powerful members of institutions and organizations within a country expect and accept that power is distributed unequally."[35] People from different countries and cultural backgrounds have different experiences with and perceptions of power distance.

People in societies exhibiting a large degree of power distance such as Latin American, Asian and Middle Eastern countries accept a hierarchical order in which everybody has a place and which needs no further justification. In societies with low power distance, such as the United States, United Kingdom and Israel, people strive to equalize the distribution of power and demand justification for inequalities of power.

Author Maya Hu-Chan writes: "Working cross-culturally is a lot like driving in a foreign country for the first time. Go on autopilot too quickly and you can easily crash and burn, too."[36] Whether you are working in other countries or employ people from different ethnic and sociocultural backgrounds, becoming aware of intercultural differences will guide you in building collaborative relationships that demonstrate respect for diversity.

Empower Women

Just as supporting DEI is good business, so is supporting women. An analysis by the Peterson Institute for International Economics of more than twenty thousand firms in ninety-one countries shows that there's a 15 percent increase in net revenue margin associated with moving from zero to 30 percent inclusion of female leaders.[37] Credit Suisse also found that companies with greater participation from women at the board or top management levels see higher returns, valuations and payout ratios.[38]

There are several ways managers can support equality, including by evaluating performance fairly, creating work flexibility, ensuring women are credited for their ideas and voice and challenging the "likeability penalty."[39] The likeability penalty shows up in our perceptions of successful men and

35. Hofstede Insights, "Country Comparison: What about the USA?" retrieved on November 20, 2021, https://www.hofstede-insights.com/country-comparison/the-usa/.

36. Maya Hu-Chan, *Saving Face: How to Preserve Dignity and Build Trust* (Berrett-Koehler Publishers, 2020).

37. Talent Intelligence, "6 Financial Arguments for Workplace Diversity," Talent Intelligence, May 1, 2017, http://www.talentintelligence.com/blog/6-financial-arguments-for-workplace-diversity.

38. Credit Suisse, "Press Release," September 23, 2014, https://www.credit-suisse.com/about-us-news/en/articles/media-releases/42376-201409.html.

39. Lean In, "8 Powerful Ways Managers Can Support Equality," Lean In, accessed August 14, 2021, https://leanin.org/tips/managers.

women. When a man is successful, his peers often like him more; when a woman is successful, both men and women often like her less. I've seen many a female leader get 360-degree feedback mentioning that she should "be less rough around the edges" and "soften her style." This trade-off between success and likeability can create a double bind for women. If she is competent and direct, she doesn't seem nice enough. If she has a softer, less direct style that is "nice," she is considered less competent.

Through social learning, we come to expect different behaviors from men and women. We are okay when a man is direct and forceful, but we expect women to be gentler in their communication. This bias often surfaces in the way women are described, both in passing and in performance reviews. When a woman asserts herself—for example, by speaking in a direct style or promoting her ideas—she is often called "aggressive" or "ambitious" (seen as "negatives" for a woman). When a man does the same, he is seen as "confident" and "strong." In this way, the "difficult" female is often passed up for projects and promotions.

Some companies counteract this bias by having leaders partner with HR in talent management meetings in order to listen for and point out potential biases. For example, if a woman is being considered for promotion to a position which requires travel, someone may say, "But she has a family so she may not be a good fit for that role." An "unconscious bias detector" would call this out ("Would we ask this question if we were considering a man for this role?") and mention that the woman needs to make that decision, not the company. If a woman is marked as a "corporate climber, out for herself," someone could point out that this behavior is encouraged in men and should not hold someone back from growing in the company. If a woman receives feedback that she needs to improve her executive presence, it's important to consider what standard of executive presence is being used. A global, diverse standard or one based solely on the pre-sentation of White male executives? Expanding our standard of executive presence would welcome more diverse and authentic leadership styles.

Other ways to support women are by encouraging flexible and virtual work options. I remember the first time I walked into the offices of Johnson and Jennings General Contracting. I observed that one of the project engineers, a new mother, had her tiny baby in an infant seat next to her. "All she does is mostly sleep and I've got to feed her once in a while!" the cheery project engineer said to me. Donna Vargo, the President and CEO, told me that she wanted to create a comfortable workplace that supports women. Hurrah for leaders like Donna!

Many of us have probably observed a woman make a statement or share an idea in a meeting, only to be greeted by silence. Within the hour, a man will repeat the woman's idea and receive credit and praise for it. This sexist conversational behavior happens enough that there's even a term for it in our lexicon: "hepeating." Another term that has become common is mansplaining, when a man patronizingly explains something to a woman that she already knows.

Being aware of these dynamics and behaviors is the first step. Talking about this with men, many of whom are well-intentioned and unaware of these habits, addresses and helps to reduce this behavior. In some groups, others will notice it and speak up. "Yes, that's the idea Luisa shared five minutes ago, and I support this."

Last but not least, it is important to raise women's awareness of the Good Girl Syndrome (also known as the Nice Girl Syndrome), a socially constructed way of being with an expectation that women will always smile, be pleasant, not rock the boat and not ask for what they deserve. A Stanford University study[40] reported that the most desirable adjectives to describe women were *compassionate, warm, cheerful, soft-spoken* and *loyal*—all qualities of a "*good* girl." When the same study participants were asked to list desirable adjectives for men, they wrote *independent, assertive, dominant* and *decisive*. Apparently, women are most desirable when they are soft and men when they are strong. Your female employees may not be asking for the positions they want or negotiating because of this dynamic. Be aware of this and empower women to speak up in the talent management process. Additionally, educating all involved about these common biases can help to prevent them, thus promoting more diversity in your workplace.

The Generation Ahead

Whether you are reading this book in 2022 or 2032, know that there will always be an upcoming generation whose needs should be considered

....

40.   Linda Babcock, Sara Laschever, and Deborah Small, "Nice Girls Don't Ask," *Harvard Business Review,* From the Magazine (October 2003), accessed August 16, 2021, https://hbr.org/2003/10/nice-girls-dont-ask.

when designing your company culture. At press time, millennials, also known as Generation Y—people born between 1981 and 1996, according to Pew Research Center—are estimated to comprise 75 percent of the global workforce by 2025.[41] For years we've been hearing, "The millennials are coming! The millennials are coming!"—They are. They are here and Gen Z and the generation after that are just around the corner.

We must be agile and inclusive to those who make up the current and incoming workforce. Before assuming that the next generation just wants more pay, a straight line to the top and cushy hours, ask some questions. Do your research before buying into the hype (and often, the negativity that exists about the future, including the new generation). How did they grow up? What are their strengths? How can they make a difference? Remind yourself that their place in history has shaped who they are and what they expect.

Millennials want to know about your company vision and values, how ethical you are when it really counts, how you give back and how you drive your people and the company forward. Millennials rate the importance of a culture fit at 8.5/10 and about 60 percent of them consider learning and development as extremely important in a job.[42] Almost 50 percent of millennials say that the opportunity to change the world motivates them to be successful.[43]

Today's Generation Asks

- What difference are you making in the world?
- Are you trustworthy and ethical?
- Do you care about your people?
- Do you value diversity?
- Does your culture feel inclusive and welcoming to all?
- Will I receive training and coaching?

41. Workstars, "What millennials want from work: 7 research-backed truths," Workstars, accessed May 17, 2021, https://www.workstars.com/recognition-and-engagement-blog/2019/10/21/what-millennials-want-from-work-7-research-backed-truths.

42. Jonelle Lesniak, "The millennial perspective on company culture," THRUUE Inc., September 21, 2017, https://www.thruue.com/thruue-points/culture/millennial-perspective-on-company-culture.

43. Mike Perlis, "What Do Millennials Want From Life?" HuffPost Blog, June 2, 2016, https://www.huffpost.com/entry/what-do-millennials-want-_b_10257926.

Flex with Flexible Work

Since the COVID-19 pandemic, most companies who continued to thrive did so with a remote workforce. Employees were hired virtually; teams collaborated without ever meeting in person; and CEOs grappled with when, how and if staff should return to working in person. You may miss the hustle and bustle of employees walking around and hearing new ideas from casual run-ins in the hall or cafeteria. You may miss the camaraderie of a team of people being together in the same physical space, running projects and creating new plans. You may also wonder if, in the long term, people will be as productive. They can be—with certain protocols in place. I advise clients to make sure employees can still meet in person at some point to strengthen their relationships, which makes collaboration easier. It's harder to ignore communications from someone you've gotten to know well. Following are considerations that may ease the transition to a remote or hybrid workforce.

Set Tasks and Deadlines: The more clarity there is around what tasks are due, when, how tasks will be done and by whom, the more successful you will be. Defining and tracking progress on milestones makes life easier for everyone. Yes, it does take time to define these milestones on the front end, but you will be glad you did in the long run. Ensure that your people have the technology and tools they need to track their work and know where accountabilities lie.

Prevent Us versus Them: If you have some employees working in the office and some working virtually, given the way human dynamics go, it can be easy to develop "us" versus "them" silos. To address this, talk about shared goals in a way that values everyone, whether they're working from the office or remotely. Encourage your people to share concerns about where the remote or on-site work team is having challenges.

Create a Collaborative Environment: As you form new teams, ensure that there is clarity on each team member's skills and how their efforts connect to the company's overall strategy and specific expected outcomes. When it comes to working from home offices, normalize talking about people's work space. What room are they in? What do they like about it? Normalize and welcome children or pets making "guest" appearances by walking by or walking in. Ask your team to share what their best hours and tips are for deep work when they focus on working strategically and developing new ideas.

Another technique to encourage a feeling of cohesion is having guidelines that can catch problems early. For example, set consistent expectations for meetings, whether face-to-face or virtual, regarding how people show up and how they are expected to contribute. Some meetings may be via conference call while others may be better with video. Make your expectations clear in advance so everyone can plan accordingly. Pay attention to body language and encourage others to do so. Our monitors are all we have sometimes and we have to make the best use of them.

Some companies designate an online coffee hour or happy hour that's just for hanging out and chatting. People may resist at first. Don't give up. People enjoy the social aspect of teams, and getting creative can help make that connection happen. Lastly, know that more than ever, your team will appreciate one-on-one meetings. Supporting people in the individual ways they need is vital.

As you consider your next steps, remember that the new normal will take time to form and there is no quick fix. It will take consistent effort to operate with expanded mindsets and practices. Check in with yourself about questions such as:

- What is important to you about having people physically in the office?
- While working remotely, what has been important for the company in terms of company goals, purpose and vision?
- How can you empower individuals to determine what works best for them?
- What value do face-to-face meetings add for customers?
- If some staff work remotely while others work from the office, how will you handle differences in perception and expectations across the team?
- What would be the cost of ending virtual work?
- What risks are there for your employees going elsewhere if they do not have the option of virtual work?

The four primary Culture Cultivators are (1) develop employee abilities; (2) communicate direction and change; (3) value people: diversity, equity and inclusion; women, minorities and generations in the workplace; and (4) flex with flexible work, which may mean new ways of showing up for you and your senior team. The techniques of the *WALK IT*® *model*, found in the fourth section of *A Powerful Culture Starts with You*, can be used to help your senior team start, refresh and update environmental changes that strengthen these Culture Cultivators.

The next section, DRIVE IT®, shares a coaching model that empowers problem-solving for you and your team members. It gives an opportunity to place your busy life on pause so you can discover where you may be stuck and how you can reflect and create new possibilities.

PART 3
TAP INTO THE ROOT OF YOUR POTENTIAL: ON WISDOM, POWER, RESILIENCE AND GRACE

Let the waters settle and you will see the sun
and the moon in your own reflection.
—Rumi

"We're here in life to learn and to teach," I hear all the time from Dr. Jackie, an 85-year-old African American woman who mentors me. Dr. Jackie is a former leadership development executive who has been involved with organization development around the globe for over four decades and now coaches entrepreneurs.

For as long as I've known her, her signature style has included immaculate-looking colorful or leather vintage. Today is no different. She's wearing a light blue leather blazer from the '70s that looks brand-new. We're meeting for lunch at a hip New American restaurant with blaring '80s music. As she gets comfortable in the booth, she leans forward and asks, "What is new with you?"

"I'm really enjoying working with my coaching clients! I've developed a coaching model that can be used for thinking through a goal someone may want to take on."

"What is your reader's need and what will you be sharing with him or her?"

Taking a pause while I pick up an asparagus fry, I reply, "Even the smartest people can get stuck in patterns or habits. And they are busy—too busy. There's always something to do. I want to give leaders a chance to pause and reflect so they can see what's holding them back and what's possible."

We are both silent for a moment. Dr. Jackie responds softly, "That is what people need today. I've been around for a minute and this I know: It is critical for leaders to take time to reflect."

The DRIVE IT model is about slowing down for a moment and going from doing to being so you can tap into your inner world and discover your potential in order to drive change. It's about discovering what you want; what, if anything, is stopping you; and how to get moving. You will learn how to examine your thinking around an issue and how to shore up your resilience for the journey ahead. This section is about the Self.

You deserve a time-out to reflect:

- Where am I?
- Where do I want to be?
- Where is the gap?
- Where do I start?

The DRIVE IT® Model

I designed DRIVE IT to give leaders steps to walk through that are simple and straightforward for driving personal transformation. This model can be used for self-coaching or coaching others through a challenge. The DRIVE IT model guides and supports you in taking charge of your life and creating a plan for something that is important to you, whether it is a work dream, a vision for your personal life and relationships, or a fitness goal. It is an opportunity to take a time-out for reflecting, dreaming and planning to make a vision or dream come true.

The steps of the DRIVE IT model help you move toward identifying and working on your goals with reflection, courage, resilience and an understanding of your inner self. Working through these steps will empower you with the clarity you need to deconstruct an issue and reflection exercises to create possibilities for your future. You will learn how to gain clarity about what is bothering you; to understand what you want and what it would be like to get that; to explore how your current mindset is serving or limiting you; and how to step outside your comfort zone and find people who will support you. This section is about tuning in to your intuition to discover an unarticulated vision or an idea you've been playing with in your mind; or to get to the source of a nagging feeling you've been having. Use the DRIVE IT model as a tool to help you think through an issue, to understand where you are stuck and to make a plan to get unstuck.

The DRIVE IT® Model	
Determine the challenge	What do I want to change? Where is the gap between where I am right now and where I'd like to be? Where do I want to be different? How do I want to be better? How can I honestly own what I think is unfortunate and what I want right now?
Reflect on what making this change would mean to me	What would be different? What would I feel like if I achieved this goal? What have I tried? What has worked? What is the vision that will drive me in tough times?
Invite a new way of thinking	How have I been looking at this issue? What assumptions do I have? Where might I need to be more humble? Where might I be assuming the worst of others? How might I view this issue from another angle? Is there an alternative explanation?
Valiantly get out of my comfort zone	Where do I need to take a risk? What would I need to give up? How do I find and tap into my courage?
Engage supporters	Who else has dealt with this? What resources are out there for me? Who can help keep me accountable? What tools do I need for success?
Initiate the first step	What is the first step I can take to get this moving? How can I make this step as easy as possible?
Transform my thinking to prepare for challenges	How can I transform my worries into hope and resilience? What might I need to give up?

WATCH IT, DRIVE IT, WALK IT: How the Three Models Work Together

Here's how to benefit from the steps in these three models:

1. **WATCH IT** to check in on and get a sense of your culture and environment; to identify areas for improvement.
2. **DRIVE IT** to do the inner self work needed when you have a personal or professional challenge and want to make a change in your life; to refresh and expand your mindset when you're stuck and want to discover a new vision, embrace a change and just go for it; to coach yourself or someone else through a personal or professional challenge. (This model can also be used as a standalone tool for reflection and driving personal transformation.)
3. **WALK IT** to create a high-energy, engaging and sustainable culture and environment, using your updated mindset.

At the end of this chapter is a fuller set of coaching questions for each step of DRIVE IT (Table 9). Use these regularly to help you to tap into your wisdom, power, resilience and grace. It will also enable you to aid others in tapping into their best selves.

Following are the steps to reflect on as you DRIVE IT. Each section provides case studies and resources and tips for walking through each step. May peace, joy and success be with you as you explore your Self.

Determine the Challenge

The first step of the DRIVE IT is to name the challenge you are facing. Sometimes what we're up against is obvious. However, there may be times when a situation is bothering you, but you aren't sure if you're in the right, or, what exactly bothers you about the issue, or if it's even worth pursuing.

What's in my head?

-   Get creative and explore your thoughts. You can do this by making time to:
-   Go for a walk.
-   Engage in activities you love.
-   Look at the situation with a beginner's mindset; be curious and put judgments on pause.
-   Stop, drop and breathe. Stretch.

An acquaintance of mine told me she rarely had time to exercise because she had a one-year-old. I asked her if she'd considered power walks with the stroller. "I don't want to do that, because then I'd have to think about my life." Ouch! Behind that comment was likely some fear—perhaps not only the fear of naming what bothered her but even more so, the fear of whether she would have the power to do something about it. We can find ourselves in a space where we grapple with an issue for a long time before we find the readiness, courage and hope to start doing something about it. And that's okay. You can start slowly. There are things you can do to start naming your feelings and to get a grip on where exactly it is that you are stuck. Sometimes it takes realizing, little by little, that you've been neglecting your voice or your well-being. Sometimes you'll have a lightbulb moment.

Jan was a talented consultant whom I'd gotten to know professionally. She had been married for over a decade and was always very put together with a short haircut and simple, elegant work suits. We lost touch for a few years and the next time I saw her, I was blown away. She greeted me in a flowy floral top, a long sweater coat that went past her knees, slim black pants and tan ankle boots. Her wavy hair flowed past her shoulders. Astonished and excited, I said, "Oh, my God, Jan, I love your look! How have you been?"

She smiled, looked into my eyes for a beat and said, "I've changed my whole life and I'm so happy now. I got a divorce. I'm working for an entertainment company and I've taken up playing the drums." She was exuding joy and I sensed major liberation vibes.

"Tell me more!" I said, as we sat down in a quiet corner of the coffee shop to catch up.

"I was at a women's luncheon for an organization that supports women in transition," she said in a more serious tone. "One of the ways they support their clients is by helping them to escape emotionally and physically abusive relationships."

Where is this going? I wondered. How did being at this event contribute to her transformation?

"They shared with us some definitions of abuse so we could understand and support the women, should we choose to volunteer for the organization. As

I read the definitions of emotional abuse on the PowerPoint slides—yelling, rejecting your thoughts, gaslighting and making you doubt your thoughts and feelings, public embarrassment and bullying—the hairs on the back of my neck stood up. I suddenly felt freezing cold, very sad and extremely angry. I had an out-of-body experience."

I stayed still and let Jan continue, not wanting to interrupt this moment of deep sharing.

"I realized that I was in an abusive relationship. I saw how I did not have a voice. My ex-husband did not want to hear my opinion, and if I shared it, he would abuse me emotionally and verbally. He'd tell me I had a mental problem, that I was taking things too personally, that I was spoiled or weak. I had to suppress my voice, my desires and hopes so as to not upset him."

As I listened to how Jan had suffered, my chest felt tight and my heart started beating faster. Learning about Jan's suffering was heart-wrenching.

She inhaled deeply and stared at the dark wood table. She breathed out slowly, as if to let those negative memories out of her subconscious. "A light went on for me that day. I was at a point that I was ready to receive this message and to do something about it. I started making plans for a different life—and I made it happen!"

We were silent for a moment as we considered her journey. We shared a knowing smile. She'd found her voice, her power, her place in the world.

"I'm so happy for you, Jan."

"Me, too! And I'm loving how I've been helping other women find their voice."

Jan's personal journey has always stayed with me. By paying attention to what was coming up for her, she was able to make vital changes and tap into her full expression. As a result, she is living a fuller life and showing up as vibrant, confident and self-expressed. This will impact the rest of her life and everyone with whom she interacts. This means it will also influence the culture she creates at her new organization.

You may share my awe of how this moment happened for Jan. You may also be wondering, "How can I make sure I'm hearing my voice, that I'm taking time to pause and pay attention to my experiences?" We can plod along in life, even being successful in our careers—not realizing that we can do and be more. Life presents opportunities to see ourselves and it is our choice if we take them or not. These realizations come when we take moments to rest, to exercise, to care for ourselves, to pause and reflect. This can let what is bothering us bubble up to the surface so we can get in touch with our inner voice and intuition. Getting in touch with your inner world begins by taking time to be still.

"Oh, no, you're not going to tell me to meditate or do yoga, are you? I've tried that—so boring!" That may be part of your journey one day, if you're drawn to it—but let's aim for small manageable steps. The more you clear your calendar for self-care, exercise and rest, the more likely new insights will emerge for you, contributing to the discovery of what is bothering you.

I'm going to share some ways to get started. I only ask that you try each one a few times to observe the impact it has on loosening your mind, thoughts and body. They may even make you feel relaxed, especially if you pair them with deep breathing. Following are some ways to become still and tune out the noise:

- Listen to relaxing music. You can find lots of good options online. Take your pick of guitar, piano, nature sounds—there's so much to choose from.
- Take a walk in your neighborhood or around a park without listening to music, talking on the phone, or checking your messages.
- Play with a pet.
- Go to the park and observe what is around you. Let yourself look at the plants, flowers and trees up close.
- Flip through travel or art photo books.
- Take your lunch and eat it at a park—slowly, no phone, just you in nature.
- Go somewhere relaxing with a journal and pen or pencil (I love mechanical pencils) and write down whatever comes to mind. Aim for filling up one page to start and go from there based on how you feel.
- Write down the messages your gremlins and saboteurs, also known as your ego, are telling you.

♟ Zoom In

How do you take time to tune in to your thoughts and feelings?

_____
_____
_____

What activities help you to relax, feel calm and one with the world?

_____
_____
_____

If you haven't taken time to relax your mind, consider what may be stopping you. What is a small first step you can take?

_____
_____
_____

➴ Zoom Out

- How might taking time-outs for reflection and rest benefit your relationships?
- How might working on personal challenges impact your mood and mindset at work?

Reflect on What Making This Change Would Mean to You

Twenty years from now you will be more disappointed by the things that you didn't do than by the ones you did do. So throw off the bowlines. Sail away from the safe harbor. Catch the trade winds in your sails. Explore. Dream. Discover.

—H. Jackson Brown Jr., P.S. I Love You

Nina, a successful and powerful executive, wanted more out of her time. Her VP-level marketing job with a large retail company was satisfying and exciting, even though her boss was demanding and sometimes difficult. Nina felt blessed that her husband supported her career and helped out with the kids.

"I'm always 'on' at work. My boss is super smart and tough, but I'm always learning. The problem is that I come home so pooped that I have little energy to be with my kids. I don't like it. I'm not happy with myself and I know I can be better. Being a good mom is so important to me and I'm not sure I'm doing a good job right now."

When I asked Nina to share more, she told me that she would come home and basically flop on the couch and watch her recorded shows. Wanting to envision how this plays out for her, I asked, "Nina, can you walk me through exactly what happens when you walk in through the door?"

"Okay. No judgments, right?" I sensed that she was carrying some shame around what she was going to tell me.

Nina said that after the initial hugs and hellos from her kids and their nanny, she goes into the kitchen and pours herself a glass of red wine. The nanny follows her in and updates her on the children's day. The nanny then takes the kids back upstairs to play, finish their homework and bathe. Nina goes into the living room and watches her TV shows, often with a second glass of wine.

"Is that so bad?" she asked, tears welling up in her eyes.

"No, Nina, it isn't!" I answered. I felt so much compassion for her. I wanted to give space and time to let her process and feel her emotions, but I also didn't want her to misinterpret my silence. "Can I ask you a question?"

"Yes," she said, wiping her nose, followed by a deep breath.

"How would you like things to be? Describe what a perfect day could be." I invited her to reflect on a different future.

"I would come home by 5:00 p.m. and instead of going into the kitchen, I'd go upstairs to the playroom. I'd sit on the couch and listen to Jane give me the updates. The kids and I could have a welcome home Capri Sun. I would snuggle with them and read their favorite stories. I actually love doing that and I love bath time. I'm feeling excited just planning this. I can even come up with easy meals that the kids could help me prepare. I've got it!"

It was recharging to watch Nina share how she'd like things to be. As she talked, she sat up straighter, her voice became louder and more energized and she smiled. It was as if she was already there. This is the power of encouraging someone to reflect on and picture the outcome they want.

Manifesting Your Dreams

Reflect on what making a change would mean to you! When you can visualize or in some physical way make yourself feel like you have reached the dream, it somehow tricks your brain into accepting it. When you accept something in your mind, it's on your mind more and you begin to attract it.

When Jim Carrey was a struggling actor, he famously wrote himself a check for $10 million for "Acting Services Rendered." He said he'd drive up to the Hollywood Hills and stare at the city lights and imagine he'd made it. He carried that check until it was tattered. And before the date on the check, he was offered $10 million for the film *Dumb and Dumber*.[44]

Michelangelo envisioned the sculpture *David* so vividly that he said he would chip away at the marble so he could uncover the person within. These are examples of manifesting your thoughts.

Try these activities to help you imagine what it would be like to achieve your dream:

- Write a letter to yourself dated two to three years from now. In the letter, congratulate yourself for having achieved your hoped-for milestone. Write the details of what is different in your day-to-day life, your relationships, your work with your colleagues and clients. What energy is around you? How are people responding to you?
- List the traits you will have gained if you reach this dream. For example, someone who is working on speaking up and sharing her voice might write: "I am self-expressed. I am confident. I am powerful. I am successful."
- Create a vision board with images, quotes, phrases and words that describe your future self.
- Share your dream with the world. Tell people; put it out there!

....

44. *Dumb and Dumber,* directed by Peter Farrelly (1994; New Line Cinema).

- Write all the things you want on a small notecard, place it in your wallet or bag and look at it every day.
- Respect the visions and images you've created for yourself and silently give love and appreciation when you see others who have what you desire. Think, "Good on you," and acknowledge their diligence and success.

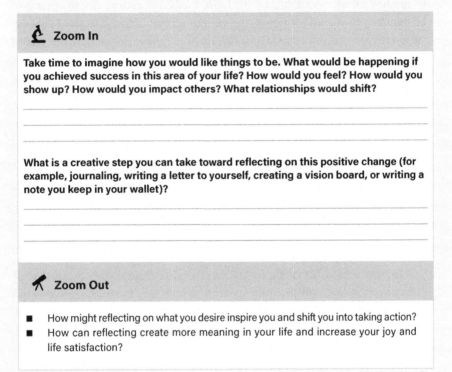

🔬 Zoom In

Take time to imagine how you would like things to be. What would be happening if you achieved success in this area of your life? How would you feel? How would you show up? How would you impact others? What relationships would shift?

What is a creative step you can take toward reflecting on this positive change (for example, journaling, writing a letter to yourself, creating a vision board, or writing a note you keep in your wallet)?

🔭 Zoom Out

- How might reflecting on what you desire inspire you and shift you into taking action?
- How can reflecting create more meaning in your life and increase your joy and life satisfaction?

Invite a New Way of Thinking

In times of distress, you may believe there is only one path between here and there. But if you slow down, you may see there are many ways to get from here to there. The paths emerge when you release fear and embrace your wisdom.

John worked in his family business with his older brother Ken. Their communication styles were so totally opposite that employees wondered how the two men were even related. John had a soft approach; Ken was direct and straightforward. Ken had joined the business a year ago and the transition had been jarring and disruptive. When it came to decision-making, Ken would state what he wanted and John would feel intimidated and walk out of the conference room to escape the stress.—Day in and day out. The tension was so thick for John that this situation was a literal pain in his neck. His neck ached, his chest was tight, he clenched his fists and he felt stuck.

In my first couple of sessions with John, I asked questions about what role he may be playing and if he was seeing the whole picture. He would shrug. He shared that conflict made him uneasy and he was not usually the one to initiate important conversations. I knew that he was the key to changing this scenario and I planted seeds by asking questions such as, "I wonder what other possibilities can be?" and, "How do you think Ken sees this situation?"

The two brothers, of course, drove the family crazy. John vented to his siblings and mother on an almost daily basis. "Ken's such a jerk! I'm tired of feeling emotionally bruised. I wish he would change! Why can't he be different?" During one of these venting sessions, his sister Grace stopped him mid-complaint and asked, "John, what do you want?"

"I want freedom and peace and joy. I have no joy. I hate this. And our brother will never change." After shedding a few tears of frustration, John realized that he was seeing himself as a victim. His sister's question, coupled with our conversations, enabled him to invite a new way of thinking about the issue. He realized that he wanted to be right. He wanted to be the golden child. He wanted other people to fix the problem. He basked in the empathy and being the "poor baby." He wanted his brother to look bad.

He called me and told me he had arranged to meet with Ken. "What should I do?" he asked.

"Be your authentic self. Remove your defenses and be vulnerable. Nothing else has worked, right?"

He tossed and turned that night as he thought about Grace's simple and powerful question. He wanted peace and the ability to flow in his work with Ken. He realized that no one else could fix this. Not his sister, not mom, not his brother. He needed to take responsibility to make things right and to get out of this messy, painful situation. "I'm in charge here and I don't need anyone but me" was a challenging but liberating realization for John.

The next day at the coffee shop, when John saw Ken approaching, he was overwhelmed by emotion. He had planned to say sorry and "Let's start over." Instead, he went toward Ken and gave him a hug. Ken was surprised and slowly returned the embrace.

From that day on, John chose to move forward with positive intent. Instead of John assuming that Ken had copied Grace on an email to make him look bad, he'd remind himself that perhaps there was a nonmalicious reason for his action. He worked on sharing his voice. He decided that only he could change the challenges in his life and he was sick of being a victim. Change was up to him.

The truth is, in times of distress, we want someone else to be in the wrong, to be the bad guy. We think, "If this person or that circumstance could change, I'd be happier." The reality is it's up to us to change. If we don't change, we'll face the same challenges over and over again. It's distressing and predictable when we keep getting the same results when we respond the same way to the same situation or stimulus. At some point, you may realize that something needs to change—and that something can only be you as you are the only person you can control or change. When John changed the way he thought about himself and his situation, he was able to experience joy and freedom and have a better relationship with his brother. If you are feeling stuck in a particular situation or relationship, where might you need to invite a new way of thinking so you can get unstuck? What biases and assumptions might you be carrying?

John had several implicit assumptions; for example, that he had a good communication style; that he must be right overall, if he was getting sympathy as the victim in this scenario; that it was Ken who needed to learn how to communicate. John learned through his deep inner work that he wanted to go from "if only" thinking to "curious and growing" thinking. "If only" thinking can lead to being doggedly stubborn about your point of view. You make up stories and invest in these narratives, acting as if others are wrong while you are in the right. You reject others for their different ways of communicating and showing up and wistfully think of what life would be like if the person miraculously changed and acted like someone else, someone they are not.

When we are in this frame of mind—which can be heightened with feelings of drama, distress and catastrophizing fears—we project our negativity onto others. We assume that they have poor intentions and judge them based on thoughts we may have about ourselves. It's a weird space in which there are no winners and the more you push, the more resistance you encounter. By contrast, having curious and growing thinking means that you are secure in expressing your thoughts and being open to others.

Going from "If Only" Thinking to Curious and Growing Thinking

When inviting a new way of thinking about a difficult relationship, ask yourself if you are defaulting to reacting and judging where you:

- Make up stories and assume negative intent in others.
- Believe these stories.
- Assume you know what others are thinking.
- Dream of other people changing while you continue on in the same way, with the same thoughts and responses.

Curious and Growing Thinking Entails:

- Being open to learning what others are thinking and feeling.
- Learning how your behavior impacts others.
- Taking the risk to share your view.
- Encouraging others to share their thoughts and being authentically curious about their perspectives.

Pause for a moment and take a few deep breaths as you think about what it could look like to operate from a place of curiosity, assuming positive intent and giving others the benefit of the doubt. It could look like calm presence, curiosity, speaking slowly and smiling. It could feel like wisdom, peace, self-confidence, detachment from outcomes, empowerment and openness to possibilities.

I see "if only" thinking all the time when clients have a conflict with a colleague. When you invite curious and growing thinking, you are moving away from an accusatory approach and seeking an alternative explanation. You can go from:

- "He's impossible!" to, "Perhaps I can connect with him in a different way."
- "She's making my life miserable," to, "I need to get a handle on my emotional responses."
- "He's taking balance out of my life," to, "I need to start speaking up, so we can get on the same page."

When we make assumptions about others' behaviors, we usually assume the worst. Call it the amygdala hijack or the fight-or-flight response. In moments of anger or desperation (add in not being physically at your best, sleep-deprived, hungry, etc.), you may make a quick negative assessment of a situation or person. According to Byron Katie,[45] to help us review our assumptions, create a new way of thinking and open the door to more possibilities emerging, we should continually ask four questions:

1. Is it true?
2. Can I absolutely know it's true?
3. How do I react when I think that thought?
4. Who would I be without that thought?

I would add a fifth question:

5. Is there an alternative explanation?

Let's see how the absence of inviting a new way of thinking can impact a whole company and its culture.

Assumptions Negatively Impact Culture

When I speak with staff to learn about a company's culture, I often see patterns of behavior centered around assuming the worst of others. This can result from our protective mechanisms kicking in. Under stress or perceived threat, we quickly leap into fight-or-flight mode. "How dare she call me out in a group email? I'll show her." "He didn't ask me to speak at the meeting. What's his agenda? What's his problem?" "He asked me to present so last minute. Doesn't he respect my time?"

....

45. Byron Katie, *Loving What Is: Four Questions That Can Change Your Life* (Three Rivers Press, 2003).

In scenarios like these, you may feel your heart racing and your chest tightening. Thunderbolts crash overhead as you plan your revenge. But if you were to slow down and pause, you may recognize that you're viewing this situation from a lens of threat and fear. From years of experience with clients and in my own life, I can tell you that, in general, people are not out to screw you over. They're dealing with their own stuff and you may happen to get some blowback from that without malintent on their part. If you learn that someone actually has it in for you, know that by confronting the person, while still assuming positive intent, you can learn more about the person's intentions *and* demonstrate that you do not appreciate the behavior.

One way to practice communicating without assumptions is by using the Situation-Behavior-Impact model[46] mentioned earlier. In this process, the communicator describes the situation; explains the behavior just as it happened, with no assumptions or assigned meanings; and finally discusses the impact for the recipient, whether toward themselves or others. Perhaps you will see yourself or your colleagues in one of the following three scenarios where the leaders invited a new way of thinking by sharing their thoughts with their colleagues.

Marc was tired of Zaynab calling him out in group emails. We discussed his using SBI to communicate with Zaynab. We made sure that Marc would be centered and relaxed before the conversation (he liked listening to Hawaiian music) and prepared to go with an open mind and positive intentions.

Marc shared with me how the conversation went: "Zaynab, on Tuesday, you sent a group email regarding our project. In that email, you detailed three items that my group missed. The impact it had on me, if I'm to be honest and vulnerable, is that it embarrassed me. It also didn't account for the whole story."

Marc described the look on Zaynab's face as surprised. She apologized and acknowledged she needed to slow down and seek more information before sending out emails. Her intent was to problem-solve quickly so they could move on to the next phase of the project. Marc took ownership of not keeping her in the loop and encouraged her to call anytime. They

....

46. Center for Creative Leadership, Situation-Behavior-Impact.

agreed to have weekly check-ins. Marc learned to share his voice and to stop assuming the worst in people.

Yasmin was angry about not being part of the team tasked with presenting a new product to their client. When she had an SBI conversation with Tito, the project lead, she was surprised at the response.

"You do such great work, Yasmin!" Tito said. "I've noticed that you've been so stressed out with all your client work and I didn't want to add to the pressure."

Yasmin realized a few things that day: first, to stop assuming ill will; second, that she was valued; and third, that she needed to manage her executive presence as it could have unintended consequences. Yasmin told me that when she was stressed, she wouldn't chitchat with her colleagues; she felt her appearance went from a put-together business casual look to something a bit messier; and she didn't smile. "Of course, I'm sending some 'stay away from me' vibes!"

Tabitha told me that she hated the last-minute invites her colleague Greg sent. She found them to be rude and disruptive. We discussed how she could put her judgment about this on pause and approach Greg from a place of curiosity. She asked Greg if there were any way he could give her a bit more notice.

"I wish, Tabitha! I get these requests last minute myself. What can I do to support you? If you can't do it, we'll work around it, but I'd love your participation."

It turned out that Greg was not a disorganized colleague. He was doing his best to arrange things so their team had a chance to share their project and the areas in which they were innovating. "It's such a good forum to share and exchange ideas and I don't want us to miss the opportunity, even if we get an invite last minute," he told her.

Tabitha felt relieved and enlightened on how approaching someone with an open mind can clear so many things up.

As you think about how you are viewing situations, you can ask yourself some questions:

- Is there a pattern?
- Where have I seen this before?
- How do I honestly feel about this situation?
- Have I played a role in it?
- Where am I in my readiness to change or take action?
- Where might I be too attached to an outcome?
- Is there an old me or old identity I want to shed?

 Zoom In

Do I take ownership of my part or do I blame others?

_____

Do I check my assumptions?

_____

1. Is it true?
2. Can I absolutely know it's true?
3. How do I react when I think that thought?
4. Who would I be without that thought?
5. Is there an alternative explanation?

 Zoom Out

- How might the absence of reflecting inward impact the system I'm working with (whether it's a family system or company culture)?
- Might I be role-modeling the wrong behaviors?
- Might I be reinforcing the type of thinking that leads to not taking accountability?

Valiantly Get Out of Your Comfort Zone

Miguel, a CEO of a commercial furniture company I was coaching, had a personality that valued harmony and consensus. This style had helped to create a warm, family-oriented type of culture with a positive emphasis on employees' well-being and work-life balance. Miguel demonstrated the same nurturing spirit with clients. This style worked—until it was time to speak up and maintain boundaries.

A client had requested a shipment of office furniture in timelines that Miguel was not comfortable with. His fear: "The client will fire us if we don't comply with the deadline they want." But the downside of saying yes outright and not negotiating timelines was that the product would be rushed, which risked errors being made. Another issue was that it would impact commitments to other clients.—All roads leading to the potential consequence of being fired by customers. Fear can be quite an instinctual, visceral feeling; you are in danger and need to respond quickly to become safe. It leads to reactionary leadership.

Miguel met with the client and they talked about their families, golf, new landscaping and home updates. (Miguel is great at creating and maintaining relationships; he always remembers what clients have told him about their activities and kids.) When the conversation transitioned to the project, the client told Miguel that she wanted the deliverables in four weeks versus eight. Miguel knew that there were ten other small- to mid-sized deliverables due to other clients in that timeline and a couple of employees already needed to work overtime. He told me that his palms were sweaty and his mouth dry. What he wanted to say was, "I'm so sorry, but we don't have the capacity to do it this quickly, because it will negatively impact our other clients. Can we get creative and see if there might be another way?" But Miguel was afraid that the client would back out and that the deal would fall through, so instead he told her, "Okay, we'll make it happen." And he told himself, "I'll figure it out with my team when I get back to the office."

If you struggle with negotiation and worry about disappointing someone, these situations can be the worst. You open your mouth but just can't say what you need to. You smile and nod, not wanting to disrupt your client's wonderful infectious energy. Gulp. You return to the office with a tightness in your chest and call an emergency meeting. What should be a celebration turns into a chaotic fire drill.

As Miguel told four of his managers that they needed to contact their clients and have a "we're pushing your deadline back" call, their faces fell.

They went from happy to sad, one by one. "I felt so demoralized," one of them told me later. "Last week's meeting was literally all about the importance of customer service. What happened?"

What happened was that their CEO's style fostered amazing service in some ways and totally neglected it in others. Speaking up was not comfortable for him and, in his mind, carried too many risks. Negotiating was "not his style." He was Mr. Nice Guy. There are roles that we come to adopt in our lives that get reinforced over time because they've brought a degree of success. But they can also be what leads to our shadow side and holds us back.

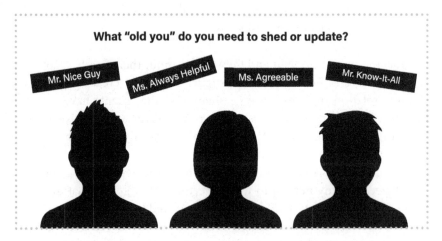

When we have a persona or identity that has worked in many ways for many years, doing anything different feels like risking losing a part of ourselves. The person needs to take a step back and see that this is just one aspect of self, a part of their persona—not their entire identity. They don't have to give up everything that they are—they can modify that aspect of self. This makes change possible and easier.

The work I did with Miguel centered around identifying how he had become so valued for saying yes, being agreeable and not negotiating. Miguel's understanding style was something he had learned and practiced from a young age; there was real value in his ability to create harmony with his five siblings and be a mediator, which he had been doing from childhood to the present. In the workplace, he was often the glue for employees experiencing conflict. When Miguel got involved, everyone walked away feeling understood and understanding one another. Managers told me Miguel had the Midas touch with people. I started by acknowledging this strength: "I'm curious about what you do to help people get on the same page."

"I listen to all sides. I have each side share what they feel and what they heard about the other side. I ask them to think about things with a new lens. I'm kind of a coach to them. I don't really tell them what to do," Miguel responded.

"How do you apply this lens and ability when you're the one having a problem?" There was silence.

"I've been so focused on doing it for everyone else and empowering everyone else. I have my clients share their thoughts, too. My thoughts are absent. I guess I'm used to being the mediator. I wish I could share what's on my mind."

"What if you could?"

"I wouldn't feel so nervous to speak up. My clients would understand my point of view and that I'm trying so hard to help them. I'd stop disappointing my team when I ask them to push client projects back. But I'm not comfortable with that approach. It just doesn't feel natural to me."

I shared with Miguel that change can happen in a series of small steps; the point was not to make him a different person but to ensure that his voice was heard. He suggested that a small step could be to tell the client something like, "I look forward to collaborating with you on how we can support you and your customers. We are here to serve you and our other clients and if we can both focus on flexibility, that would be tremendous."

After trying this a few times, Miguel said that it was getting easier to speak up about deadlines that were too tight or that would negatively impact other customers. He also took time before meetings to reflect on the other customers his team had brought on and how he did not want to disappoint them. This inner work helped Miguel inch out of his comfort zone toward a learning zone and experimenting zone.

To get out of our comfort zone requires looking deep within to learn about our own assumptions and values. Miguel unknowingly had an assumption that speaking up for himself was not "who he was." Once he realized and checked this assumption, he chose to take small steps to practice a new way of being, one that added to his style instead of requiring him to halt his style.

New ways of being, such as speaking up for oneself, require a new mindset followed by learning and finessing new techniques. Mostly, it requires courage. To feel your neck heating up, your palms sweating and a tightness in your chest and yet hold a vision of what you want to push forward and go in the direction of your discomfort is being brave.

Choose a Symbol or Metaphor

Sometimes a symbol or metaphor can help nudge you toward the learning zone. Kamala wanted to remember to negotiate tasks (instead of saying yes to everything) and to delegate and coach (instead of doing everything). She made a sun symbol in her notebook before meetings, as a reminder to get out of her comfort zone to negotiate timelines and delegate tasks. Her daughters are her sunshine and she wanted to keep the vision of spending time with them in mind, as a motivation to change.

Create Time to Think

Matt was a brilliant vice president who received feedback that he needed to be innovative, forward-thinking and the leader for bringing in new ways of serving existing and future customers. Matt said that when he put forward new ideas, he would be barraged with comments like: "We tried that five years ago!" "Clients don't always like that type of technology," and "That's pretty expensive!" He understood where this was coming from but also felt like he was hitting a wall. "Over half of the senior team members have been at the company for more than ten years and act like there's 'nothing new under the sun,'" Matt told me. "I feel like I'm ready to stop proposing new ideas. The resistance really drains my energy. As is, I barely have enough time to think these ideas through because of my other responsibilities."

Matt was struggling, because he was so accustomed to being agreeable and getting on the same page with his teams. There were two issues here: First, Matt needed time to think through his ideas. Second, Matt's inability to engage with conflict and talk about ideas without getting defensive or shutting down had to change. Both these issues required Matt getting out of his comfort zone.

We started with a calendar review. Matt realized that he spent 20 percent of his time in meetings that didn't absolutely require his involvement. He decided to delegate those meetings to his reports who could then share updates with the team. This could contribute to their growth and give him more time. Next, he wanted to work on the "constant interruptions" that resulted from his open-door policy. He established office hours in the morning and late afternoon. In between, he closed his door for two hours a day for creative time—reallocating the 20 percent time he saved from not attending every meeting. He let everyone know the purpose of this time: innovating. "I felt guilty at first, but it's getting better," Matt said. "People are getting used to it. They are also seeing that they can carve out concentration time." He also came up with a plan to gather industry journals, research industry trends online and touch base with colleagues.

Speak Up without Shutting Down

The second part of Matt's work was around engaging with resistance nondefensively. He redefined "being on the same page" with someone as collaborating versus being in total agreement. He started wearing the "researcher" hat as he came up with new ideas. He took the risk of sharing his thoughts with his colleagues in one-on-one settings to get their buy-in. It was clear that he enjoyed coming up with ideas now that he had the space for it. "I'm taking off the Mr. Agreeable cape and putting on a cape that reads Inventor."

As the weeks went on, Matt presented his ideas with a calm pace and was welcoming of diverging viewpoints. He started seeing the differences as a good thing versus a reason to run. "I felt brave and calm in our last meeting," he told me over Zoom. "The senior team had concerns and it was okay. I listened, but I didn't shut down or back down. They want to make sure we're doing the right thing—so I stayed with them. I got feedback that I was open, focused and spoke with passion. We're taking next steps toward a new technology!"

🔬 **Zoom In**

What persona has been driving your comfort zone?

_____

_____

_____

How does this persona help you?

_____

_____

_____

How does it hold you back?

_____

_____

_____

How can you update your behaviors to get better outcomes?

_____

_____

_____

What "old you" might you need to shed?

_____

_____

_____

🔭 **Zoom Out**

- How can getting out of your comfort zone help your company thrive?
- How can it help you better serve customers?
- How will it help you innovate?

Engage Support

There are times when you're trying something out or taking on a new venture and feel overwhelmed and don't know exactly where to begin or what to prioritize. You need help (and you may even need help to be able to articulate that)!

When I decided to launch Strategy Meets Performance, I had to go downtown to get my business license. The administrator asked me if I wanted complimentary mentoring as part of the services offered when you get a business license. "Huh?" I asked, feeling a little run-down and ragged from the late nights of working on proposals and marketing communication.

"You'll get matched with a retired executive who worked in your field and can support you in launching your business."

Someone to help me navigate this new world? Um, yes please! "That sounds great, I'll take it!" I told the administrator.

The SCORE (Southern California Office of Retired Executives) mentor assigned to me was Dr. Jackie. What a godsend! I love her relaxed, Zen-like energy. As we have spent time together, I've learned that she's rarely surprised by anything I tell her—from my challenges in learning business development to making sense of social injustice in the world, to navigating family drama to managing networking colleagues who show inappropriate behavior. She also laughs a lot and helps me laugh at myself. The best is when she replays what I say so I can hear myself. Sometimes there's nothing as satisfying as re-viewing how ridiculously I've been seeing a situation. Everyone needs someone who can, in a loving manner, poke holes in their arguments and views, especially when they are self-righteous. If you are open to it, it's one of the funniest things to chuckle at yourself—your old self of five minutes ago.

Why am I sharing my love for my 85-year-old cool, wise, slick mentor? Because I attribute much of my increased wisdom over the last decade to her. More importantly, it's to check in with you, my wonderful reader, to see if you are able to accept support or to recognize if you have hang-ups about asking for help, as many driven, high-performing people do. When you go it completely alone, it creates unnecessary work and inefficiency. Why re-create the wheel when you can gain support and achieve your goals faster?

Great athletes don't achieve success alone. Aside from having coaches, fitness trainers, nutritionists and sometimes sports psychologists, they also have loving family members who are supporting them, traveling with them and cheering them on. Your city council person, mayor, governor and president didn't get there on their own either. When we see someone who is wildly successful, we may think about how hard the person has worked and persevered. We often forget that behind many successful people is an amazing team, an amazing family. As you've probably heard, "It takes a village."

"I have big goals. I need a team behind me," can seem like such an obvious thing. But as an executive coach, I know this is not always easy to practice, even when we know support is "a good thing." Many people resist asking for help for a host of reasons, including negative self-talk, and as a result, struggle more than is necessary, re-create the wheel and lose valuable time toward achieving their goals.

Six Reasons We Avoid Asking and Keys for Reframing

There are six common reasons why people resist seeking help.

1. *Pride, pride, pride.* You fear coming across as needy, unable, or incompetent.
2. *Quid pro quo, oh no!* You don't know what favor the person may want at a later time.
3. *I hate hearing no.* You fear the person may reject your request.
4. *It's too big a request.* You don't want to burden the person.
5. *It's been too long.* You've lost touch with your friends and associates and may feel silly calling because you need help.
6. *Maybe I'm not ready.* You don't really want to change or take on the goal or project.

Being aware of these factors and how to reframe them through asking yourself pivotal questions can empower you with insights to view the resistance differently. When you can examine and deconstruct your struggle, you can become more open to taking a small step.

Pride, pride, pride: Consider: Where have you learned that seeking help is equated with being helpless? Did a parent or family members have an attitude of, "I don't need anyone's help?" Did you see someone "over-ask" for help and take advantage of others? Although it's great to be sensitive and considerate, know that most people like to help.

> *Reframe:* When was the last time I helped someone? Do I think people who ask for help are needy? What might be another way of seeking help? Where's the line between seeking help and taking advantage of others?

Quid pro quo, oh no! Okay, maybe now you're thinking of yourself and the worst-case scenario of someone asking you for something financial or totally unreasonable or unethical. This is where it's important to create and maintain your boundaries. Honestly, what's the worst favor from a normal, well-adjusted person likely to be? Contribute to my charity of choice? Support me at my event? If you're that worried about taking a favor from someone, maybe the person has some shady qualities that make you nervous. In that case, follow your instinct and maintain boundaries.

> *Reframe:* Reflect on if there is an opportunity to help the person out in some way. What if, to ease your concern, you were to get clear on a quid pro quo; for example: "Let's edit each other's blogs"?

I hate hearing no: So you fear rejection? Ask yourself how big your favor is. Is it reasonable? Is it hard to manage? Does it create a conflict of interest? Does it ask someone to get totally out of her comfort zone (like asking someone who hates giving speeches to speak at your event)? If the answer to these is yes, go back to the drawing board. If no, ask yourself, "What's the worst thing about being told, 'Sorry, I can't help you right now'?" Explore where and when you may have been told no or didn't get help. How did you feel? Rejected? Unloved? Embarrassed? Okay, that happens, especially when we don't have a context for how to make sense of the world around us.

> *Reframe:* Where did you learn to fear being told no? How can you acknowledge it and decide to take a different approach now? What pleasant opportunities might asking open up for you, even if the person can't help you? What are your thoughts around boundaries? Did you see a parent or family members who lacked boundaries?

It's too big a request: You may think your request is too big. If so, consider breaking it down into smaller parts and ask the person for what you really need. Instead of, "Can you help me with my presentation?" ask people to help with smaller chunks, based on their interests and talents. Maybe you can ask one person to review your outline, another person about whether your deck is visually appealing and someone else to give you feedback as you practice delivery. For example, I always offer to review press releases, bios, blogs and other written materials. I'm good at it and it's easy for me. Find where people's talents lie and show appreciation for their efforts. Also, instead of a boring ask, put some humor into it: "Do you know someone who is amazing at ruthlessly critiquing decks?"

> *Reframe:* How big of an ask is too big? Might it be possible to pay the person or barter with something you can do? If you ask around and try to divide up the request without success, might there be a need to hire a professional?

It's been too long. You may have a friend or contact you haven't kept in good contact with. Calling and asking for help may feel silly or disingenuous. Start with an email or text to schedule a coffee or lunch—or, if you feel comfortable, pick up the phone. Rekindle the vibes and have fun. See what you can help the person with. Sincerely offer your support. Then, after another get-together or call, or seeing each other, follow up and ask.

> *Reframe:* Maybe I can check in and see how my friend is doing and make it less about me at this moment. What if I'm the person my friend needs to talk to at this moment? Recall the traits you really appreciate about the person. Ask yourself, "What is the worst that can happen?"

Maybe I'm not ready. You may have used the first five ways to resist seeking support and I've hopefully helped debunk some of those fears. Now it comes down to the crux of the issue: maybe you're not ready to ask for or receive help.

Tom, a colleague, asked me how things were going on my book. He offered tips on writing and self-publishing—all great stuff ... that I was not ready for. A year later, we spoke and that information was exactly what I needed to hear. If people have offered you help and you didn't take them up on it, it could be that you have some more work to do on your project, rendering the wonderful support unhelpful at that time.

One way to work through any of the six reasons we avoid asking for help can be by engaging the support of a few friends or a "mastermind group" who can help you challenge the messages you give yourself. As I was writing this book, I certainly had some messages to boulder through, such as: "I'm so busy and have so much to do." "There are so many books out there; will this book make a difference?" "This process is sometimes boring!"

The impact of this self-talk was negative, because it kept me stuck. How could I feel inspired or driven to hustle and consistently work on this project, week after week, month after month, when I was thinking about it as lacking in joy, fun, or excitement? When I shared this with my group, the members supported me in naming and reframing the negative messages I was sending to myself.

Message: "I'm so busy and have so much to do."
Reframe: "What's more important than this? This will be a dream come true!"

Message: "There are so many books out there. Will this book make a difference?"
Reframe: "There is always room for more knowledge and this book has not been written using my voice. I can help so many leaders."

Message: "This process is sometimes boring!"
Reframe: "There are some things that are fun about the process of being an author, like the creative process, designing a cover and getting it out into the world. Yes, editing and rewriting can be boring and tedious and that's okay."

Confronting my self-talk was a huge key to getting inspired to write every day, even if I wrote just a page or jotted down some ideas. Try this reframing technique to rev up your project!

I hope that by this point, you are starting to discover your deep well of power, wisdom and confidence. There's a world of support, reciprocity and community out there for you to gain support and give support.

🔬 Zoom In

How did you see people helping others growing up?

_____
_____
_____

Was helping others seen as a joy or a burden?

_____
_____
_____

Do any of the six reasons people don't seek support resonate with you?

_____
_____
_____

Where did you seek or get offered help that made a big difference for you?

_____
_____
_____

When did you help someone who was grateful for the support?

_____
_____
_____

🔭 Zoom Out

- What might it be like to be part of a community that's exists solely for the purpose of helping one another succeed?
- What are your thoughts on reciprocity? Have you ever noticed that there seems to be a natural order where help comes back around, even if it's not from the person you helped?
- How can you create or encourage a community of support?

Initiate the First Step

Sometimes the smallest step in the right direction ends up being the biggest step of your life. Tiptoe if you must, but take the step.

—*Naeem Callaway*

Whether you have a big difficult problem or a persistent challenge buzzing around you like a mosquito, taking the first step requires wrapping your head around the actual issue. Using the DRIVE IT model so far, you've gotten an idea of how to **D**etermine what the actual challenge is and **R**eflect on what making a change would mean to you. You've **I**nvited a new way of thinking about your challenge and questioned your assumptions. You may have examined your tendency to jump to worst-case scenarios about taking risk. Perhaps you've learned to put on your curiosity hat when you confront shady behavior from others and rather than assume that the person has negative intentions, recognize that maybe their behavior is not about you at all. You've **V**aliantly decided to get out of your comfort zone and negotiate that deadline or express your idea. You've figured out why you may have had hang-ups around seeking support and have found a way to **E**ngage support.

And here you are: On the edge of **I**nitiating the first step.

What's that now? You have some jitters? There's some self-talk popping up? Maybe your mind is telling you that you don't know what you're doing or where to start? That's okay. Let's talk through this:

You may be hesitant about initiating a first step, because you think you don't know what you're doing. So? Where did you get the idea that you came into this world programmed and equipped to know how everything works? Although not having much information can feel daunting, it can also be an exhilarating time of discovering and learning.

Think of the first time you tried a new sport. You may have felt awkward and clumsy about the moves or the lingo. In skiing, for example, there's so much to know about the boot fit, the ski length, how tightly or loosely you'll be bound into the ski, etc.—And that's before you even get on the slopes and figure out how to get on and off the lifts, while all around four-year-olds are swishing down the mountain without any poles. Still, something has compelled you to get out there and you're motivated to figure this thing out. Maybe you prepared by watching a video online or talking to friends. Maybe you just showed up—the most important part, hey! And, bit by bit, you start figuring it out; you gain skill and confidence.

Sometimes I ask clients: "What did you feel was keeping you from taking that first step?" They often respond to this question with comments like: "I didn't have any instructions. I was partly winging it until my company came together and I hired my first employee." "I thought I was going to make mistakes as a first-time mom, but I did fine. My husband and I always figured out what we needed to do. We'd read up online and ask our friends." "I broke the task down into small parts and that made it more manageable every day."

Think about times when you started a new job. There may have been a lot to deconstruct and reconstruct and you did it. Often there is an opportunity to make order out of chaos or structure out of seemingly unrelated information. Make a list of all the times you walked into ambiguous or undefined situations and created a system, steps, or methodology. How did you break things down until you achieved your goal? If your list doesn't convince you that you have the skills, curiosity and resourcefulness to figure it out, then ask your partner, family members, friends or colleagues about times they've seen you figure out a challenge.

Think of one small step you can take toward your goal. One phone call, one coffee with someone, one visit of a website, one conversation with a friend. How can you make this goal fun? Can you work on it outside? Can you brainstorm with a neighbor? A client really enjoyed taking some of his "creativity time" at a coffee shop and exclaimed that he could not believe how much work he got done in a different environment. "It's a nice way to unplug from the office and be away from the typical distractions! The noise-cancelling earbuds do help though!"

Creative Ideas to Get You Going

Creative activities can help you to get started. Here are a few ideas for starting steps that can be fun, different, or even soothing. They may help you to release some of your anxiety or lead you to another activity that will help get you going. One step is often all you need to create momentum.

List It out: Brainstorm a list of activities you can do to get the ball rolling. Let's say you have to create a presentation and are feeling sluggish about starting.

List the things you'll need to do to create a compelling, positive, high-energy talk. Your list may include creating an outline; finding a nice design; selecting images; doing research, etc. From this list, pick one easy step that can be fun, like looking up images or finding your design template.

"Why Do I Suddenly Feel Like Cleaning?" Who cares? Do it! Let's say you've created a list you feel good about, but you're still not feeling that *vroom* that gets you moving and in the zone toward your goals. You may decide that before you can take a step, you need to clean your closet, coordinating by color and moving aside clothes that can be donated. Oh, and your garage feels like it needs a bit of organizing.—That's okay, go for it! Of course, there's a load of laundry that needs tending to. Elizabeth Gilbert, author of *Big Magic*,[47] encourages you to do all the things you need to until you've literally run out of tasks and are now face-to-face with yourself—in a clean, organized space.

"Get Your Butt in Seat": Whether you're writing an article, a book, or new ideas for your company or presentation, getting started can feel like the biggest drag. All of a sudden, everything else seems more important than this important task. "Get your butt in seat" is a term I've heard used a lot in writers' circles. It's about creating time and then literally getting your rear in your seat in front of your computer or notebook. What I've heard from successful authors about how to start writing is: Craft time to write each day, for an hour or even less. Just sit down in front of the screen, or with a notebook if you like to write by longhand. This way, you are letting a process emerge. Inspiration is more likely to come when you give it time to show up.

Detach from the Outcome: When we are overly attached to outcomes, we are unable to be our most creative selves. How can great ideas emerge when you are filled with anxiety and dread about everything that could go wrong? The more you're able to focus on the task at hand, the freer you will feel to work on the task. We know that much learning in life comes from the process and the journey, not the destination. The art of life is about embracing this.

Just Ten Minutes: What if you told yourself that all you need to do is work on your goal for just ten minutes at a time? Ten minutes of writing ideas,

....

47.   Elizabeth Gilbert, *Big Magic: Creative Living beyond Fear* (Penguin Publishing Group, 2016).

doing research, pulling out files, organizing.—Set a timer and get started. Whatever happens after that is pure bonus. You might feel compelled to do ten minutes more and maybe another ten minutes after that. (You can apply this technique to other areas, like getting back into exercising. Ten or twenty minutes a day is all it takes to get started.)

Change the Scene: A great way to get started on a task is to take your work out of the office, if you can, and get into a new space—preferably one that is sparse and simple. In pre-pandemic days, people working at the office could benefit from taking their work to a conference room or a small breakout room. Many people love coffee shops. The reason changing the scene works is that you don't have your usual things around to distract you. No books to sort through, no files, no laundry and no veggies to chop for dinner prep. I'll often bring a journal I've been wanting to thumb through or my local paper to get me started. If what I'm working on requires a bit of research, I'll print some items in advance so I can read them with ease, highlighting and making notes as part of my prep. If you can swing it, sometimes the best place for creativity can be a hotel room. I've joined my family members on occasion when they've had work conferences and it was hands-down the best place for me to focus. Since many of us work from home, perhaps trying out a different space in your house, kitchen, or backyard, if possible, can give you some of that oomph that comes from having a change of scene.

Honor Your Own Art, Ideas and Innovation: When you start something new—whether you're an entrepreneur coming up with fresh ideas or a leader trying to figure out a strategy for tapping into a new market—you are starting with a blank slate, like an artist. Tell yourself you need time to work on your craft and protect your time. As you play with ideas and have starts and stops, remind yourself that art emerges and that it's not always easy.

Protect Your Time: Producing new work requires the right setting, tools, timing and mindset. Many authors share that the biggest obstacle to creative work is not protecting their time. Carl Newport[48] argues that the best way to get more meaningful work done is by working deeply—working in a state of high concentration without distractions—on a single task. He shares how throughout history, the best writers, inventors, politicians and

....

48. Cal Newport, *Deep Work: Rules for Focused Success in a Distracted World* (Grand Central Publishing, 2016).

artists had a habit of protecting five hours of their day for deep thinking and deep work. They would use these sacred hours for their craft only. It makes sense. Think of the times when you've wanted to concentrate on an important task. Aside from the usual distractions, you've likely had phone calls and people coming in and out of your office, or now home office. To successfully create your art—be that working on the company strategy, assessing and making a plan for your talent, or creating a persuasive pitch—you need to protect your creative time.

Treat Yourself: Once you've gotten going, find little ways to reward yourself for completing your milestones. Perhaps that's watching an episode of your favorite show if you spend two hours on your task. Or promising yourself that if you spend five hours on your task, you'll get yourself frozen yogurt at your 3:00 p.m. break. Ask your partner or a family member to check in on you, as an accountability partner. Promise a family member that you will take them to a nice dinner when you're halfway through your project. These may sound like silly mind games, but they work. I've promised myself that I will go to the mall with my husky at 5:00 p.m., if I've finished editing the final section of this chapter!

🔬 Zoom In

How does your work setting help you to perform deep work?

_____

_____

_____

How might your work setting inhibit you from performing deep work?

_____

_____

_____

What nonessential yet helpful things can you complete before diving into your important project?

_____

_____

_____

🔭 **Zoom Out**

- What are three ways you can protect your time?
- What are three challenges you have with protecting your time?
- How can you get support to protect your time?

Transform Your Thinking to Prepare for Challenges

As you begin working on your goal, you will have ups and downs. You'll laugh, you'll cry, you'll give yourself high-fives. There will be times you'll want to quit. I've had plenty of moments of wanting to throw in the towel and flop on the couch. "Why is this so hard?" I would ask myself through these difficult times. At times I would remind myself of what I've accomplished so far as well as countless feats and successes my clients have shared with me that they cannot believe they accomplished.

After getting through these times and learning how clients have stayed on track despite many challenges, I've identified that expecting and embracing the tough moments and—crucially—transforming them are the keys to resilience when you face the slammed door, a no, lack of interest and the fatigue of working hard without results.

Expect It

As you work toward your goals, knowing and expecting that there will be those moments when you want to crumple the project and make a basket into the closest bin, or to quit in a screaming fury will help you to prepare. One branch of philosophy that is relevant for expecting challenges and imperfection is stoicism.

Stoicism is an approach that helps us direct our thoughts and actions in an unpredictable world. Since we possess limited control of external events but have some actual control over our mind and behavior, stoicism helps us to be more resilient and thrive through life's storms, rather than being torn down by them.

Around 304 BC, a merchant named Zeno was shipwrecked on a trading voyage and lost everything. Making his way to Athens, he was introduced to philosophy, which changed his life. In later years, Zeno would joke, "I made a prosperous voyage when I suffered shipwreck." He would gather regularly with his followers to teach and discuss philosophy, logic and ethics at the Stoa Poikile, or "painted porch"; this is where the word "stoic" comes from.[49]

The four virtues of stoicism are courage, temperance, justice and wisdom. This philosophy has been practiced by great leaders, artists, writers, politicians, soldiers and entrepreneurs throughout history, including Marcus Aurelius, Frederick the Great, Montaigne, George Washington, Thomas Jefferson, Adam Smith, John Stuart Mill, Theodore Roosevelt and General James Mattis.

This philosophy seems to be reemerging in modern society and reminds me of elements of emotional intelligence, resilience practices and mindfulness. You may think that stoicism means becoming a person who can endure pain or hardship without showing their feelings or complaining. It is much deeper, however, and more helpful than it may seem at first. Stoics believed that their way of viewing the world would prepare them for anything.

The Little Book of Stoicism[50] presents some practices that I believe are essential for creating an expectation for obstacles and challenges in your journey toward greatness:

"Beat fear with preparation and reason."[51] More often than not, the things we fear most don't happen, but we spend a lot of energy worrying about and projecting all the things that could go wrong in the future. One of the reasons for this is that we become too attached to expectations and outcomes that are beyond our control. "We fear because we want what's outside our power, or we're too attached to something that's not in our power to keep. ... And we desire what's not in our power to receive."[52] Just as you can expect that you will have fears, know that you can overcome them by thinking through the situation rationally, calmly and often, until it becomes familiar and even boring. Confronting these fears will reduce the stress. For example, ask yourself: "How likely is it that I'll become homeless if I don't succeed in this project,

49. Daily Stoic, "What Is Stoicism? A Definition & 9 Stoic Exercises to Get You Started," Daily Stoic, accessed October 16, 2021, https://dailystoic.com/what-is-stoicism-a-definition-3-stoic-exercises-to-get-you-started.

50. Jonas Salzgeber, *The Little Book of Stoicism: Timeless Wisdom to Gain Resilience, Confidence and Calmness* (Jonas Salzgeber, 2019).

51. Salzgeber, *The Little Book of Stoicism*, 182

52. Ibid, 183.

or get that promotion, or grow my business?" Maybe you remember that you ran another meeting, which was meh and didn't get the engagement you wanted, but the sky didn't fall. Get feedback and try again. Your best antidote to fear is preparation and staying focused on and positive about what you can control. That's it. If you stop expecting that things will go perfectly the first or second time around, you'll be more resilient and more at peace.

See pain as an opportunity. People often see adversity or pain as some-thing negative that thwarts them from reaching their goals. How can you turn this around and see the challenge as an opportunity for growth? Pain actually means something is happening beyond the zone of comfort (where there is an absence of pain as well as an absence of achieving greatness).

What's happening in the here and now? When you have multiple projects and are feeling stressed and anxious about the future, take a mindfulness break (take a walk, get a coffee, sit outside for ten minutes) and allow yourself to zoom out and get some perspective about what's happening in the moment. Is the project really out of control? Are you actually failing (whatever failure means)? The past has occurred, the cookies irretrievably fell on the dirty con-crete, the car got dented, the conversation did not go as you planned. It's over. Forgive yourself, take a break and make a new plan for right now—rather than jumping into "terrible future mode," predicting how your life might be impacted. All is not lost and you are capable of fixing this.

Embrace It

If reaching your goal were easy-peasy, everyone would be doing it. When clients tell me something is hard, I acknowledge that not only is trying a new behavior challenging, it's supposed to be! If what you're working on is perfectly aligned with your natural energies and you have the skill and time to work on it, then we don't really have a problem, do we? When you're pushing yourself out of your comfort zone, expect to experience some pain, self-doubt and resistance. It's okay! It means you're growing! It may be stretching you to learn a new skill you never had before. It's okay to own the fact that what you're doing is really freaking hard.

If you want to grow, go ahead and select your struggle. Success often requires struggle and grows from solving problems. The sooner you decide what it is you are willing to struggle for, the easier the struggle will become, because you've named it and owned it.

We've all heard the cliché, "No pain, no gain." Think about all the ways you've triumphed and all the pain that went along with that. Was it worth it? The more we can embrace that stress, drama and anxiety will be part of the process, the less we may be actually impacted by these things. You know it's coming, it doesn't mean you're "failing," and you can prepare yourself with short- and long-term strategies to handle these situations and care for yourself.

Transform It

Can you imagine taking the angst, fear and ambivalence of starting a new project and turning it into something awesome (in addition to accomplishing the goal)? What if you could learn about yourself during the process and grow your resilience and wisdom to the point where they're useful for future projects and, believe it or not, one day, useful for helping others with this challenge you've conquered?

The Tale of the Pedestrian Crosswalk

There was a thoroughfare near my home that made safe pedestrian crossing impossible. Designed like a highway, the road ran through two neighborhoods, and cars zoomed by at much higher than the 35 mph speed limit. The sidewalks were covered by bluffs that should have had retaining walls and there was no safe access to reach the other side of the street by foot.

Knowing that there had been many near accidents as residents tried to walk to the nearby shops and restaurants and that providing a safe path for crossing for residents is a right, I decided to take action. I was driven by the vision of a safe, walkable community that encouraged getting around and visiting local businesses on foot. More than anything, I was driven by the anger and fear of innocent people getting injured or killed because of the city's negligence. There are many times when residents seek a pedestrian light in a dangerous intersection where they lack access or safety and they are ignored. That is, until someone gets killed. Then a cross light gets installed within weeks.

"Not on my watch," became a guiding vision and motto as I collaborated with my neighbors to drive this change. I got others on board and created a group of activist residents. Looking back, I chuckle as I recall that we had functions within our small group of committed resident citizens. We had government affairs, community affairs and marketing. When government officials did not respond to our request, our "marketing team" started an email drive and created a website. It generated some movement and information but no time frames for change from government officials, so we contacted the local press. We were in the local paper and the news over time. One friend noted that he saw me on the news and commented, "You were mad!" as he recalled me stating that something needed to be done or, "Someone would get hurt or killed."

There was some sort of determination in all of us neighbors that kept us attending community meetings where we shared the need for change, participating in email drives, contacting the press, showing up for interviews, going in and out of government officials' offices and hosting events. It was one of the most frustrating and rewarding experiences I've ever had. Over the years, friends, neighbors and colleagues would ask me, "How's that safety project going?" to which I'd reply with a big sigh, "It's going. We're working on it."

Looking back, I realize that what I relied on was grit—a dogged, tough resourcefulness that would not let me or my neighbors give up. I chose to be active rather than passive. I chose to be an actor rather than a bystander. I chose to do things to increase our team control and influence rather than sit on the sidelines and complain. I took initiative and directed our situation, rather than being swept along passively. We had to keep this dream alive—and it finally paid off!

After eight years of community organization, as we activated the new cross light signal and paraded with balloons back and forth through the intersection with the press snapping photos, I thought of what my father told me whenever I was ready to quit fighting. "Don't give up, don't give up, don't give up." He made me see that change was possible and failure was not an option.

When it comes to your challenge, ask yourself why it's so hard and why it hasn't been done before. You have to create a vision that will keep you going, no matter what you face. What vision can you create and what messages can you tell yourself to keep you going? Who can you get involved to support this vision?

🔬 **Zoom In**

Where have I shown up with full not-giving-up-for-nothing grit before?

_____

_____

_____

Am I demonstrating agency and tapping into my power in this situation I want to work on? If not, what can be one small step toward shaping the outcome I want?

_____

_____

_____

What message will I give myself when I feel like giving up or turning in something that is not my best work?

_____

_____

_____

🔭 **Zoom Out**

- What is so troublesome in the here and now?
- How can I grow from this?

Five Reasons We Get Stuck and How to Get Free

The DRIVE IT model has hopefully shown you how you can name and own your challenges and achieve the goal you're dreaming of by bravely taking small steps and reviewing your mindset. But you may still have some doubts about getting started nagging at you. I wanted to talk about the reality of being stuck, even paralyzed, when it comes to taking the first step after you've become aware of your challenge.

Perhaps understanding the common reasons for why we get stuck and how to turn things around will ignite your fire to get going. When you're grounded in the human psychology of what paralyzes you and others from going toward big dreams, you will have a better chance of getting yourself unstuck and helping others to do the same.

I have created this section to help you identify where you specifically feel stuck and then to learn the art of getting unstuck. As you read through, consider the feelings that come with each reason for getting stuck or not starting something and then think of your preferred future. Ask yourself questions like: When have I been stuck like this before? How did I prevail? How can I reframe my thinking?

Going toward what you want requires a combination of seeing something bigger and greater and having the courage to take little steps until you gain momentum. A great recipe for success is taking an honest look at the times you have been resilient, persistent, stubborn, tough, thick-skinned, vulnerable, joyful and fearless. How did these characteristics help you to take a step?

Reason #1: I Might Totally, Terrifically Fail

Fear of failure. We've all been there, thinking, "If I try, I may fail. If I don't try, there's no risk of failing." This type of thinking comes from two things: first, how you define failure; and second, what you perceive to be the "risk" if you "fail."

If you define "failure" as "If this doesn't work, I'll never make it in life," you will be in grave trouble, because your mind will keep you from seeing new possibilities. If you redefine "failure" as "I will put forth my best effort and if it doesn't work, at least I tried—and something better may come of it," you will go forward with a more positive attitude.

What if you eliminated the concept of "failure" from your consciousness and started taking baby steps toward your dream? In the early days of starting my business, I had a couple of wailing episodes and asked my family, "Am I going to make it?" They would tell me, "Get yourself together, Nooravi!" and my tears of fear would turn into tears of laughter. Ultimately, I moved ahead as if failure were not an option. For some odd reason, it never truly occurred to me that I might not make it. Perhaps all those statistics about the high percentage of businesses that start but don't succeed motivated me further.

What is the risk if you "fail"? What is the absolute worst thing that can happen to you? Typically, people fear the new endeavor not working out well. But whether it's taking the promotion, moving to a new location, or adding new products or services, without a leap of faith, nothing will happen and you and your company may stagnate. That's a risk, too.

There are endless examples of civil rights leaders, scientists, inventors and actors who "failed" more times than most people could handle. Walt Disney was fired from the *Kansas City Star* because his editor felt that he lacked imagination and had no good ideas. Oprah Winfrey was fired from her first television job as an anchor in Baltimore for getting "too emotionally invested in her stories." Designer Vera Wang failed to make the 1968 Olympic figure skating team. When she became an editor at *Vogue*, she was passed over for the editor-in-chief position. At 40, she began designing wedding gowns and her company is currently worth over $1 billion. Thomas Edison was fired from his first two jobs for not being suitably productive. He went on to hold more than a thousand patents and invented the phonograph, an incandescent lightbulb and one of the earliest motion picture cameras. Harrison Ford was told by an executive that he'd never succeed in the movie business, and his career went on to span six decades and includes his success with the *Star Wars* and *Indiana Jones* series. The list goes on and on.[53]

> *I have not failed. I've just found 10.000 ways that won't work.*
>
> —*Thomas A. Edison*

Had Walt, Oprah, Vera, Thomas, or Harrison let their "failures" define them, we would not have benefited from their gifts. Had they let the risk of putting their authentic selves out there stop them because of what people might think, they and the world would have missed out.

Reframe: Failing means you are learning and getting closer to your goal.

Reason #2: I Don't Know What I'm Doing

When we are approaching something for the first time, we can often make assumptions that hold us back. Assumptions about what we are not versus what we can be. Whether we want to take up tennis, improv, or business development, we may tell ourselves, "I'm not an athlete, comic, or

53. Rachel Sugar, Richard Feloni and Ashley Lutz, "29 Famous People Who Failed before They Succeeded," *Business Insider,* July 9, 2015, https://www.businessinsider.com/successful-people-who-failed-at-first-2015-7.

salesperson." We may also believe fallacies such as, "Only extroverts can be public speakers," or, "Only super fit people can run marathons."

The key here is to examine our assumptions and fallacies. There may be an underlying belief that you must complete ten thousand hours of practice before you can be good at something. Perfectionism is a close relative here: "If I don't do it perfectly, it won't be acceptable."

When you want to take on a bold new goal, you must understand what you'll need to accomplish this goal and then take stock of your existing strengths, abilities and energies. Ask yourself:

- What skills does it take to achieve this goal?
- Who are some people who are good at this? What do I observe in them?
- How many of these skills do I already have? What transferable skills might I have from something similar I've done before?
- What new things will I need to learn or pursue?
- How much energy do I have for figuring it all out?
- Might I need a coach who can guide me, share patterns of success and speed up my process?

Most people have more capabilities than they realize. When I visited Australia, I walked into a bathing suit shop and got to chatting with the owner, as I tend to do with business owners, curious about how people have started their business. Jeanne told me that she and her partner had zero experience in the swimwear industry, but they'd grown up at the beach and were passionate about swimwear. "So how did you start?" I asked.

"Well," she said, "we Googled 'how to start a swimsuit business.'"

How fearless is that? Jeanne and her partner had a vision and lived experience and just needed to figure out the how-tos. If you need more convincing to take the leap, perhaps you can try out a few small experiments. Do some initial research and then discuss next steps with a friend or trusted colleague. Consider contacting others who are in a similar industry and ask questions. Seek out a business coach who helps with start-ups. There are many mini-experimental steps that can get us closer to a place of readiness.

Often, though, when we have the dream in mind, we need to make a quick decision if we are going to take the leap. There was a time when I resisted starting my business. After going back to school and completing my doctorate, I applied for a job that required all the experience I had, including the degree I had earned literally two months prior. After a few interviews, I was informed that they did not see a fit. I'm normally somewhat resilient, but I was crestfallen in this instance. When I relayed what I thought was tragic news to my mom, she didn't get caught up in my theatrics bordering on victim thinking. In the most easy-breezy tone, she simply gave me instructions for the next chapter of my life: "Honey, go downtown, get a business license and put your website together." I thanked her for the advice, told her those were good ideas and ended the conversation with, "But where will I find clients?"

There were several notable things about my resistance. First, starting a company seemed daunting; there was much I would need to learn. Second, I assumed I knew nothing. Third and most importantly, I had an implicit assumption that I couldn't figure it out.

Why? What on earth? I've accomplished many things and dealt with ambiguity. What was so different this time? I'd always held business development professionals in high regard (I still do!). But I believed that they had learned superpowers over time in order to connect with clients, understand their issues and partner with them to create solutions. At that time, how this could be done was a mystery to me, like the Egyptian pyramids, Stonehenge, or the Bermuda Triangle. I also had in my head the statistic that most businesses fail in one to ten years.

Imposter syndrome—doubting one's abilities and feeling like a fraud—also played a role. Imposter syndrome disproportionately affects high achievers who find it difficult to acknowledge and build on their achievements. Some common signs of imposter syndrome are an inability to realistically assess your abilities and skills, doubting what can be possible for you, attributing successes to external factors and fearing failure when trying something new. Check, check and check.

Through a stroke of fate, I was referred to a CEO who wanted to work on creating a better culture, where employees got along and customers were treated well. I had nothing to lose as I drove to his office. No agenda or plan. Nothing specific to sell him. I knew my craft and had a few questions sketched out to learn about his situation, what was going well, what he wanted to see happen and what success would look like.

I had a great time learning about how he had built his company, all the clever things he did for marketing and where things were now. At the end of our conversation, after listening deeply and asking questions, I said: "It seems like many things are going well, congrats! I would suggest executive coaching for you and your managers, plus a series of custom development workshops for you and your team." I shared potential solutions, based on my knowledge and expertise. I wasn't following any formulaic sales plan. Someone told me later that what I'd done is called "naked consulting."

"Can you show up here this time next week with that in a proposal?" the CEO asked.

Gulp. Snapped out of the moment, I realized, Oh, wow, I *do* know what I'm doing! "Yes of course. Thank you, and see you then." And I figured it out! I was in business less than four weeks later with everything momma suggested: a business license, business name and complete website.

There are so many lessons I take to this day from that experience:
1. Make your positive talk louder than your negative talk.
2. You know more than you think you know.
3. You're smart and can figure it out.
4. There are more resources out there than you imagine.
5. You're not the first person doing this for the first time!

Reframe: Start learning and know you can figure it out.

Reason #3: The Mountain Looks Huge

A person who has done the research and knows what it takes may get frightened and believe the task is too big. It honestly makes you wonder how anyone does anything. How does someone decide to climb a mountain, compete in the Olympics, apply to medical school, run a marathon, start a business, take on a new position, become a parent, write a book, or (insert any other big, seemingly impossible goal here)?

Going toward a huge goal requires having a vision for the amazing future you want to create and breaking your tasks into bite-sized pieces that you can digest. When that future inspires you enough, it will make you okay with the struggle. You've got to be hungry!

If you've started on a change, congratulations! If things aren't moving as fast as you'd like, or if you gave up once, examine why. Did you commit to too much in a short period of time? Was the goal overwhelming? Can you break down the goal into smaller pieces so you can celebrate small wins?

The Telescope and Microscope: Big View, Small Steps
Going toward a huge goal requires two views: (1) Creating and seeing a vision for an amazing future (seeing through a telescope); and (2) breaking your tasks down into bite-sized pieces that you can digest (seeing through a microscope).

Discover Your Ikigai: Ikigai is a Japanese concept that describes someone's reason to get out of bed in the morning. In French, this may be called *raison d'être*, or your reason for being or existing. Ikigai is a combination of the words *iki*, which means life or living and the word *kai* (pronounced gai), which represents value, effect, results, or usefulness. The concept is depicted by four overlapping circles that represent:

1. What you love.
2. What you are good at.
3. What the world needs.
4. What you could be paid for.

Your ikigai is the point where these different circles come together. In other words, it's where your passion, mission, craft and calling intersect.

How does this relate to going for your big, scary goals? When you discover your ikigai, performing your work will feel more energizing, interesting and joyful than painful. Of course, there will be long hours and moments you want to throw in the towel. However, the intrinsic joy of performing the task can greatly reduce the challenge and motivate you to break the tasks down into smaller pieces. Going back to swimsuit entrepreneur Jeanne and her partner, they loved fashion, swimming and the beach so much that it drove them to design creations that others would enjoy.

When you enjoy your work, you're good at it and the world wants it, you'll have achieved the beautiful formula for success.

Reframe: Discover your ikigai and break the task into tiny steps.

Reason #4: I'm Too Busy

If you feel stuck because you are too busy, it may be for one of two reasons. The first is being busy procrastinating. Let's say you know what you need to do, you've broken the task into small bits and you're still not in the mood to take it on. You stay busy with other important responsibilities or come up with other activities that will keep you busy. We all do it. The key is how to get out of it.

As Elizabeth Gilbert says, go ahead and do all those other procrastinating activities. Clean the house, remove the excess, organize your photos, do the laundry, rearrange your kitchen cabinets. Go Marie Kondo on your space. Then you'll be left with yourself. And you'll eventually get to the task. If performing these tasks reduces your anxiety (which is what keeps you procrastinating) and gets you closer to your task, it's worth it.

The second type of "too busy" is when you're truly overwhelmed by your responsibilities and don't know how you could tackle another goal; you can't see your way out. Melissa, one of my clients, had decided that she wanted to go back to school and earn her master's degree. "How on earth will I do it, though? I have a full-time job, two kids in grade school and a household to run." At the same time, the program she was considering had many advantages: It was designed in an executive format, which meant it was for working adults. She had to attend class two nights a week and every other Saturday. Completing the program would make her eligible for promotion, which would offer more flexibility with her time. She had shared with me her worries about missing her kids' sports events and other activities.

"What would happen if you didn't go forward with this?" I asked her, attempting to see if she had the energy and verve to push forward. Without it, she could give up or fizzle out.

"This has been a dream of mine for ten years and for the first time in my life, I'm seeing possibility. I'd regret it if I didn't earn my graduate degree. It will be a huge accomplishment and I'll be so proud of myself. I can't wait!"

Once she was clear that this was the real deal, Melissa came up with ways to tap into her existing network of parents, friends and family. She discovered that her kids spending Saturdays with her in-laws was a win-win. On the two days a week when she was in class, her husband Amer would pick up their kids from after-school care, where they would have already completed their homework. He'd prepare dinner, spend time with them and get them to bed. "He was happy to do it. I feel so blessed," Melissa said. A side bonus of all of this was her husband spending more time than usual with his children and enjoying it. Melissa did have to curb her perfectionism when he did things differently, like ordering pizza or other takeout for dinner.

When Melissa graduated the program and had her kids walk across the stage with her, she cried. She told me that it's true that many achievements "take a village," but she had been so busy relying on herself that she had neglected to ask others for help. "I'm so blessed I turned to the amazing people in my life."

Reframe: Your goals are important! Get help and make time.

Reason #5: I'm in a Terrible Situation and It's Hard to Get Out

Sometimes we can feel stuck in our lives because of unhealthy communication patterns with clients or colleagues. There can be a spectrum here, anything from dealing with an annoying personality to dealing with someone who is emotionally abusive. We can feel powerless because we are stuck or not yet ready to make a move toward growth and change, or because we do not know how to access our power in a given situation.

When I started working with Kate, she had already launched her own business. She shared with me the tipping point for how she reclaimed her power. Her previous job required her to travel from Los Angeles to Chicago every Sunday night and work on the ground with her clients until Thursday night. Throughout the week, Jen, Kate's boss, would berate her in front of clients, pointing out any errors in her work, presentations, or responses. Kate was not only embarrassed but also felt that clients took her less seriously and seemed uninterested in building a relationship with her. Jen also faced negativity from these clients; some would even curse at her. Jen would appease them, apologize and get back to work. It seemed that abusive behavior was a part of the toxic culture overall. The kicker was that once a week, Jen would call Kate to apologize for her interactions.

Kate hated working for Jen and didn't enjoy the client interaction much, but she loved using her expertise in online marketing. Kate's reports also loved her and she took time to mentor them. Each Thursday, Kate would drag her weary self to O'Hare International Airport, emotionally exhausted, wondering what she was doing with her life. She would get home, unpack, sort and begin laundry and then eat and vent on the phone to her close friends. If you recall the Drama Triangle, with the roles of a rescuer, a persecutor and a victim, Jen was, of course, the persecutor and the villain and Kate was the victim. Kate's colleagues, neighbors, friends and family members who were sympathetic to her and available to listen to her suffering and offer support were the rescuers.

Kate told herself that quitting would be a shame and that she did not want to leave her team. Going to HR was not an option as Jen and the head of HR were friends. But after nine months of this, as she prepared for bed one evening, Kate was faced with herself. She cried, knowing she had to go back to Chicago in three nights.

Kate had difficulty confronting Jen in private and froze in front of clients. She shared that while growing up, she and her family members had faced abuse and were unable to speak up for themselves. We can often find ourselves repeating unresolved patterns in our lives. After several sessions with a coach Kate had hired at the time, she saw a connection between her family's abusive dynamic and her current responses to Jen. "My father was awful to us and I was resilient enough to get through that hell. I did not let him define me or stop my success. I'm strong and confident and I'm determined to get through this." She was clear on the problem but stuck on what she could do next.

After yoga one day, Kate got to chatting with another yogi about her work. Her new acquaintance's eyes lit up as she shared that she owned an online marketing firm and loved being out on her own. As Kate walked back to her hotel on Michigan Avenue, the spring tulips seemed brighter and the sky bluer. She felt a little less of the weight of the world on her shoulders. Something had awakened in Kate. She realized that by not taking action, she was choosing to be stuck. "I'm not going to be a victim anymore," she thought to herself, as she quickened her pace, taking deep breaths of air. She felt an onrush of adrenaline pulsing through her body. "I can be more than this!"

That conversation sparked for Kate the idea of going out on her own. Over the next three months, she wrote content for her website, registered for her business license and started reaching out to her network. Her Thursday nights were now spent looking up beautiful images for her website, asking entrepreneur friends for advice and planning her outfits for breakfast and lunch with potential clients. She shared that these were the scariest and most enthralling few months as she "planned her escape."

"Jen threw a fit the day I gave my notice," Kate told me. "By this time, I had worked on becoming centered and I felt like a spectator to her drama. I nodded and, as I heard the usual garbage she was spewing, I was smiling on the inside, knowing that I was free. Instead of using my resilient spirit to tolerate her, I used it to find myself and my path."

At the time Kate and I worked together, her business employed twenty people and she wanted me to coach three of her managers. As I reflected on her story on my drive home, I realized that we can get particularly stuck on what to do when facing injustice. There will be people who try to take advantage of us and project their own negativities and insecurities. It is particularly hard to escape a pattern that is familiar. Regaining your power requires some work:

- Naming a terrible dynamic can be empowering, as it gives you an opportunity to make sense of what's happening and take action.
- Being honest with yourself about the roles you play and how you and others benefit. For example, the person in the victim role of the drama triangle may get a lot of attention and sympathy; the rescuers feel like they are making a difference.
- Noticing the content of your conversations. If you are in a situation like Kate, ask yourself, "Why are the majority of my conversations centered around this person?" and, "What power do I have to shift this?"
- Tapping into your power often takes inner work like mindfulness and stillness, along with the outer work of talking to others, hiring a coach or therapist, and journaling. Talking it out can often help you to process the situation and bring you closer to freedom. Pay attention if you notice that your position in the drama triangle is not changing. Perhaps you can slowly move out of it by reflecting on what's going well and what you would like to have and by talking with your conversational partner about these questions.
- Taking baby steps, whether that's researching the area you want to move toward or joining a networking group.

Reframe: Reflect on and figure out why you are tolerating abuse. Identify your power.

Visit www.apowerfulculture.com for additional case studies and resources about other ways we get stuck and how to get unstuck.

When you feel like change is impossible, try these self-coaching thoughts on for size:

- How might this be possible?
- When have I succeeded despite great odds?
- Ask yourself: Am I the first person who is going for this goal? What patterns of success might I find?
- Tell yourself: I'm smart. I can figure this out.
- Ask yourself: If not me, then who?
- Consider if people have ever, unprompted, encouraged you toward this goal or seen great potential in you.
- Name your fans (people who think you are cool, kind and talented).

Ask yourself: What's the worst that can happen?

Rate how important achieving this goal is to you on a scale of 1-10. If it's an 8 or higher, you are probably already taking action. If it's in the 5-7 range, take time to explore, experiment and learn more. If it's 4 or below, maybe shelve it for now.

TABLE 9. Coaching Questions to Help You and Others DRIVE IT®

The DRIVE IT® Model	
Determine the challenge	What's on your mind? How is this impacting your life? What would you like to be different? How are things now? What would life be like if you could eliminate this challenge? What have you tried? What has worked? If you had a magic wand, what would you make happen for this situation? Is there anything you need to let go of?
Reflect on what making this change would mean to me	Imagine that you've resolved this issue. What's different about your life? Take some deep breaths and fast-forward to a future where you've accomplished your goal. Walk me through a perfect day. What are 5-10 words to describe how you would feel about yourself if you completed this goal? Let's move two years into the future where you have achieved this goal. What are you feeling? Complete this sentence: When I reach this goal, I will be _____.
Invite a new way of thinking	What story have you been telling yourself about this issue? What other explanation might there be for what is happening here? How else can you look at this challenge? What if you were to assume positive intent? What have you done that is working? What might you need to quit doing? If you were to take a huge step back from the trees and look at the whole forest or get an aerial view of this situation, how do you observe yourself showing up?
Valiantly get out of my comfort zone	If we put this goal aside for a moment, what do you appreciate about where you are now? How is this place helping you? What might happen if you stay in this place? How would you describe going out of your comfort zone? How might you feel if you were to take a step toward your goal? What do you think it might be like to go from a comfort zone to a learning zone? When have you achieved a goal that was initially challenging and uncomfortable? How did you go about it?
Engage support	Where might you find support? What tools do you currently have available to you for working toward this goal? How have others sought support when working on this type of goal? Might there be resources available for people who are working toward this goal? Name some people who cheer you on and believe in you. How did these supporters aid you in the past? What name can you give these people/this group?

Initiate the first step	What feels overwhelming about this goal? Where might you be feeling stuck? What are three obstacles that stand between you and this goal? If you could remove one obstacle, what would it be? Brainstorm: If you were able to break this goal down into twenty manageable steps, what could be some of the early steps? What is one tiny step you can take toward your goal (even a phone call or looking one thing up online)?
Transform my thinking to prepare for challenges	Let's imagine that you are working toward this goal. Congrats to future you! What obstacles might you face? How can you prepare yourself to be centered when you have tough days? What are the common challenges someone who is working toward this goal may face? What might be some workarounds? What might be some resources to help you feel grounded? Think of an achievement you're proud of. What were some obstacles you faced and how did you handle them? What did you learn about yourself? How can you apply that learning to the current situation? Describe a time you were working on a big project or goal and things got difficult. Share the story and who was involved and what you were thinking. What was it about your thinking that helped you with the situation?

PART 4
CREATE A POWERFUL
AND ENGAGING CULTURE FROM THE TOP

WALK IT® Steps for Creating Culture

If you're following this book's models in the order presented, you've had an opportunity to WATCH IT and learn about your company's culture, detecting strengths and opportunities and what may be stressing your culture. You've also discovered how you can cultivate the culture you want for your organization.

You reviewed your mindset, fears and things that were keeping you stuck in DRIVE IT. You've processed how you contribute to your company culture and have worked through a personal and/or professional challenge. You've also learned questions for coaching yourself and others. When you can break down a challenge, imagine a better way, get brave, get support and create a new mindset, you will be able to expand your success, skills and community.

The next step now is learning how to WALK IT. This model empowers you to walk the talk, lead an empowered team, integrate values and track what's most important. You are ready to create a strong, sustainable, amazing culture where employees are not just satisfied or engaged but invigorated! Imagine a workplace where leaders do what they say they will, communicate beautifully to every employee at every level, in every language necessary and provide the support to get to the finish line. It's not a utopian dream. It is very possible and it's in your hands.

In this section, in addition to sharing case studies of coaching clients, I've incorporated organization development best practices that apply to group dynamics, adult learning theory and ways to improve culture. Let's dive in!

The WALK IT® Model

My intention with WALK IT is to help you, the leader, entrepreneur, Culture Guardian, or management afficionado, to better understand the concepts of creating culture. The WALK IT acronym embodies what I have found to be best practices in creating a strong workplace culture.

The WALK IT® Model	
Walk the talk	Back up your words with action and be the first to practice what you preach. When you walk the talk, you take a long-term focus, lead with values, create boundaries and stand by those values as an individual leader and as part of a team.
Align your senior team	Create a safe environment where your senior team members are empowered to voice their opinions and ideas. Encourage them to debate ideas with grace and respect. As a senior team, agree to bust silos rather than create and sustain them.
Look at your culture	Take the time to observe feedback with an open mind and heart. Challenge yourself when your ego makes you defensive. Know that a strong culture where employees are heard, cared for and given opportunities to do great work will make your company a desired workplace despite turbulence in the economy, the industry, or world affairs.
Know your plan	Clarify and share your vision, strategy and values. Make decisions based on your vision, strategy and values and refer to them in big (town halls, all-employee emails) and small (daily individual and team conversations) communication avenues.
Integrate values	Successful companies have clear core values. Determine the positive behaviors that have helped your company thrive and the behaviors you will need to achieve your strategic goals in the next 3-5 years. Recruit, promote and exit people with company values as you guide your company to its north star.
Track everything	You get what you measure, and a feedback-rich culture moves companies forward. Most employees *want* to perform and are motivated when constructive feedback and coaching is delivered in a professional and caring manner. Making check-ins a regular practice with customers ensures your team is on the right track.

At the end of each step of WALK IT, you will find a set of questions to help you assess how your team is doing. I recommend that you refer to these questions regularly, because culture, priorities and team members evolve and this impacts how you are working. Checking in on these short questions from time to time can help you to stay on track and maintain your progress. Here's to you and the good health of your company culture! Onward!

Walk the Talk

One of the most difficult aspects of leadership is demonstrating the values and behaviors you espouse—and walking the talk is what employees want *most* from their leaders. Not walking the talk consistently is one of the biggest complaints employees have about their leaders in feedback interviews. Walking the talk consistently means doing what you say. It sounds simple and it is not.

You are walking the talk with your team if you (1) back up your words with action; and (2) are the first to practice what you preach. Any time you share standards with your team, you must be the first one to practice and uphold these principles. Failing to do so invites tension, disappointment and disengagement. Not walking the talk is probably the most discouraging thing a leader can do. The following case study demonstrates why it can be difficult to walk the talk as a leader as well as how to frame it and name it to follow through on your commitments.

As I sat in the cool conference room, admiring the beautiful Golden Gate Bridge, I wondered about Zeeshan's progress since our last meeting. He was a practice leader for a thriving consulting firm and his focus had remained on growing the team and creating a great culture. Two days earlier, he shared by email that he had a scintilla of doubt about his progress. "I'm not sure people are engaged. They're doing the work and meeting deadlines, but something just seems off."

I had encouraged Zeeshan to seek feedback from some of his Culture Guardians—employees who go above and beyond to protect their company culture. Culture Guardians are as conscientious and committed as if they were company owners. Zeeshan identified his two Culture Guardians as the type who "bleed the company color" and would do anything to keep the company successful. Pleased to hear about two such people on his team, we agreed that talking to them would be a great step to learn more about the current climate.

Zeeshan, fit and of average height, walked into the conference room looking like the neutral face emoji. He sat down carefully, putting his notebook, pen and water thermos to the right of his space on the table. With the afternoon sun streaming through the blinds, the vertical stripes on his face momentarily made me think of a man behind bars. Zeeshan did not look like he was enjoying his 40s at this moment.

He interlaced his fingers and jumped in. "Things are not good. I spoke with Anusha and Selena, two of my Culture Guardians. They said there are a couple of areas where I'm not following through on my commitments. I can't believe this. I feel sad, mad, offended and misunderstood. It's hard to be at the top!"

"I admire your courage for seeking feedback," I said. "Shall we unpack this?"

Zeeshan shared that he had received feedback that Marina, one of the practice leaders, demonstrated "rough behavior" toward the new consultants. Rather than redirecting their work and coaching them, she behaved dismissively, made disparaging remarks and showed her displeasure openly with eyerolls and head shakes when she found errors. The new staff especially hated asking Marina questions. "Several team members said that they were uncomfortable working with her and didn't see themselves working here in the long term." Zeeshan hadn't realized the extent of the issue and was now faced with how to handle a high-performing practice leader who brought in many clients and kept the practice humming but damaged the culture. "Look at this comment she made in an email that she inadvertently forwarded to one of the consultants."

I took a breath and scanned the lines until I got to the end where Marina had written, "I'm still cleaning up the puppies' mess at the office. What a pain. When will this end?"

Zeeshan shared that Marina's behavior violated his values of how to treat people. "Six months ago, at our holiday party, I stated the importance of collaboration, patience and treating one another with respect. Since then, I've discussed the values at each staff meeting and I've acknowledged team members who are practicing this. I want to keep these people happy and excited to be here. I also need to keep the company's successes on the up and up. I know I must act. I hate conflict, but I hate what is happening more. When I talk to Marina, she always says everything is great."

It was clear that Zeeshan was struggling with doing the right thing. He wanted Marina to behave respectfully with the staff. He was also concerned that Marina might take offense with the request to change her behavior and possibly leave the company, taking the ability to bring two million dollars in revenue a year with her. He felt like he was in a lose-lose situation. If he confronted Marina, he worried she'd leave. If he did not, he feared his high performers would leave. Getting clear on his values and working on his capacity to speak up were going to be his first critical steps toward resolving this situation.

I shared with Zeeshan that from a systems perspective, walking the talk is one of the things employees want most from a leader. Employees become disappointed and disillusioned when their leaders say one thing and do another; and eventually, high performers will leave if there's a disparity.

"Zeeshan, you've told me before that when you state the importance of something, whether it's how to treat customers or how to collaborate, every behavior and communication must demonstrate this conviction."

He nodded in agreement, ran his fingers through his salt-and-pepper hair and settled with his elbows on the table, head in his hands. "This is quite the dilemma."

"I know you're thinking that this is so obvious," I said. "You're probably also silently telling me that this is easier said than done. Am I right?"

He fidgeted and tapped his pen on his head. "Everything I've been working so hard for is being destroyed. I've stopped bad behaviors before and people always appreciated that. But this is a tough one. Have you come across this before?"

I could see that Zeeshan was breathing in a shallow way. This was no place from which to explore options for important decisions. I also wanted him to find his own solutions and was not going to tell him what to do. I asked him if we could pause for a few minutes, to take time to get centered. I played a guided meditation video to create some space for Zeeshan.

Balancing between not judging Marina (who apparently seemed to hate coaching others and wanted to focus on business development) while sharing the potential consequences of allowing this behavior to continue, I asked Zeeshan if he had considered the financial impact abusive leaders have on a business.

"Well, I'd imagine there is a time investment for counseling such leaders, legal costs if there is a lawsuit and then having to recruit and retrain new employees."

"Yep, you are crystal clear on the consequences, Zeeshan. I've got nothing to add at this moment," I chuckled.

I sensed that Zeeshan needed more time and resources to make any decision. Knowing instinctively that he was most powerful when he gave thought and time before taking big actions, I shared a values mining exercise to help him identify what was important to him so he could think through this dilemma with more clarity. As we walked out the door, he took a deep breath, smiled and said, "I'm feeling better about this. I'm going to call you next week after I've taken some actions."

Mining Personal Values

Just as it is important for a company to impart core values that guide employees' behavior, it is important to name your own personal values. Most people use values to guide their behavior. The trick is to articulate them. Doing so will give you clarity and make decision-making, redirecting behavior and managing personal resources much easier.

A week later, Zeeshan called me and shared that the values exercise opened his eyes and helped him regain his power. As a result of becoming clear on his own values, he decided to confront Marina and clarify boundaries for how she needed to respect the team. He also developed a plan for her five employees to join the other managers' teams. He shared that next, he would clarify the values and share examples of what it looks like to live them. (see Integrate Values, p.189) He had also initiated coaching for Marina with the human resources department. He said she was angry and told him coaching wasn't necessary. "I told her internal coaching was critical. I will also get her an external coach. I will work on bringing on another person to help with business development. If things don't turn around in the next six months, I am going to make a strong decision."

When you say one thing and do another, it demoralizes your team. It can make them question their desire to stay with your company. It can teach them that manners, customer service and kindness don't matter in the workplace. Taking the easy route is a short-term solution. Doing the right thing takes creativity, investment and sometimes potentially losing some revenue in the short term. The benefits are long-lasting. Walking the talk, defining your company and personal values and setting boundaries will transform your culture. Remember, you will get what you tolerate, so raise your standards and lower your tolerance.

Ask Yourself

- What are the top three behaviors I want from my team? If your values are clear and current, use these to guide behaviors. If not, review Integrate Values from the WALK IT model.
- How can I demonstrate these behaviors?
- What are the benefits of walking the talk?
- Who can I talk to when I'm at crossroads on demonstrating these behaviors?

STOP AND START
⊙ **Stop** Thinking about everything in the short term.
⊙ **Start** Considering the behavior and service you would like your company to be known for in the long term.
⊙ **Stop** Focusing on what you don't want.
⊙ **Start** Thinking about what you do want. Create plans A, B and C so you are agile.
⊙ **Stop** Being passive about behaviors you don't like.
⊙ **Start** Defining your values and standing by them. Take a risk, be confident and trust your judgment.

TABLE 10. Walk the Talk Checklist

Please note if you take the following actions consistently	YES	NO
My senior team and I walk the talk and follow through on our commitments.	☐	☐
My team has a clear accountability plan on outcomes and behaviors.	☐	☐
We have methods in place for team members to approach us with feedback.	☐	☐
I regularly seek feedback from my staff.	☐	☐
I take time to coach staff on the leadership I would like to see them practice.	☐	☐
Points to Consider ■ What could working on this step do for your culture? ■ What potential action steps should you take? **Suggestions** ■ Read *What Got You Here Won't Get You There.* ■ Seek feedback from your team.		

Align Your Senior Team

Senior teams need time to meet, not only to create strategy and discuss progress on the objectives that follow but also to have space to challenge the status quo, ensure departments are operating cross-functionally and collaboratively, brainstorm, get creative and speak their truths. A common challenge among a company's departments are silos,[54] where each department leader works independently of the others and in the process, hoards information and creates turf wars that cascade through the departments. If members of the C-suite don't get along, their teams will likely not get along. It's territorial and weird and it hurts business. It's also super common as humans tend to create and protect turf when they're

....

54. Silo is corporate speak for when different departments of an organization operate independently from one another. In farms, grain is stored in separate tall, cylindrical silos to protect it from the elements until it's ready for distribution. In companies, silos are departments with leaders who don't seek input on their strategies and neglect to see how their efforts will help or hinder those of their counterparts. Having silos typically results in incomplete efforts, confusion and a lack of clarity.

under pressure, when they're not mindful, or when there are no clear requirements for how the senior team works together. In the end, it hurts everyone. The invitation is to get everyone moving in the same direction.

Saeeda walked through the door and slammed her notebook on the conference table. Petite with her strawberry blonde hair up in a messy ponytail, a charcoal sweater over a black sheath dress and black flats, she did not look like her usual cheery self. "I'm tired. I'm sick and tired, Shahrzad. Is this what they mean when they say, 'It's like herding cats?'" I guessed she was rushing in from her last meeting, as she sat down, closed her eyes and started rotating her neck. I wanted to give her a moment to settle in. Saeeda was the CFO of a mid-sized technology company. I had found her to be a warm, strong, articulate and driven woman. On this particular day, it seemed she had reached her breaking point. Her eyes looked sunken, as if she hadn't slept well the previous night.

"Saeeda, take your time," I told her. "I'm going to step out for a minute. Take some deep breaths and I'll be right back."

Earlier in the week, Saeeda had shared that getting her team on the same page was proving more difficult than she had imagined. I had been working with Saeeda as well as Rey, her CEO, and coaching their senior team as a whole. This had several benefits. I knew the other members and the team dynamic well.

In my initial coaching session with Rey, he asked how he could get his senior team more aligned. When I shared what it would take to get everyone moving in the same direction, he said that he believed Saeeda would do a great job heading this up, plus it would be an opportunity to expand her leadership skills. After having facilitated several sessions for this team, a part of me knew that Saeeda's strengths would work better toward team alignment than Rey's. His style seemed to focus on helping each department leader versus the whole team. I noticed that Rey tended to favor his chief operating officer (COO) over his chief marketing officer (CMO). By not working with the entire group and showing how they could collaborate, problem-solve and create a clear workflow, his C-suite ended up working on their individual parts. This may have created a silo mentality among the senior staff, preventing collaboration and a systems-wide view of the organization.

Saeeda's innate ability to connect with people coupled with her love for the company seemed to make her the perfect person for bringing the team together, getting everyone on the same page and agreeing on their initiatives. But so far, things were not going well. The lack of cohesion was creating issues with providing high-quality services to clients in a timely manner. Leadership was also sending mixed messages to employees. One leader would say something; another would reject it.

Saeeda and I had initially booked this session to discuss meeting facilitation techniques. But her challenge centered around getting her senior team moving in the same direction, learning from one another and making decisions together that would benefit the whole company and not just individual departments. Saeeda shared that there was no common unifying vision bringing them together.

How Leaders Promote Silos

Leaders can inadvertently promote territorial, noncollaborative behavior by not asking for teamwork, by siding with one function over another and by not creating a clear process that ensures partnership over competition.

After listening intently, I shared a message of hope with Saeeda. "You are not alone. I see this among my clients all the time. I know we were supposed to talk about meeting facilitation, but it sounds like the bigger issue is around gaining team alignment. Would you like to focus on that instead?"

"Yes! Let's talk about how I can get everyone on the same page, with the same vision," she said with a smile.

Putting on my organization development hat, I encouraged Saeeda to ask the team a series of questions to explore what was important to the team:

- What do you think our team does well?
- How could our team work together better?
- What does each department do well?
- How can our departments work together better?
- What would be the most useful way to spend our time together?
- What is the single most important thing for all of us to be on the same page about?

"Do you think they will be open to answering these questions?" Saeeda asked.

"Learning what's working and what people need is a great first step."

"I'm feeling hopeful about doing this!" She pushed herself back from the marble conference table and stood up, taking a long stretch. She smiled, "Okay, Doc, I hope I have a lot to report on our next call."

When we spoke next a few weeks later, Saeeda updated me on the team's response to the questions. "Wow, the five of them had a lot to share! They do want to be on the same page and they're all frustrated about the back and forth between us and inconsistencies in our words and actions. Can you jump-start us as an objective external person and I can keep things going as the internal point person?"

In the months that followed, I taught Saeeda facilitation techniques and worked with the team to gain clarity on their vision, strategy and values. I helped them learn about each other's personality styles and the impact it had on their work. Ben, the COO, said he often felt pressured to agree to new methodologies without taking the time to review them in detail, which led to hesitancy in following through. "If you want me to support something, I need to understand it and help design it," he mentioned in one of the team meetings I facilitated. Tiana, the CMO, shared that she usually had such tight deadlines to develop marketing material that she hadn't been able to build in time to seek input from Richard, the head of sales. Week by week, I supported the team in speaking their truths, assuming positive intent and coming up with new solutions. They had many of the answers and needed to feel safe enough to speak their truths.

In between these sessions, Saeeda did a great job following up with team members and ensuring that initiatives stayed on track. As the team learned the WALK IT model, they would remind each other of key steps. "Hey, guys, are we aligned on this?" "Does this decision reflect our values?" Saeeda reported that the team was using their meeting time to problem-solve, brainstorm ideas and coach one another. "It's a world of difference. We learn from one another and have actually become closer!"

No More Status Meetings!

In a 2007 study of how executives spend their time, researchers found that meetings take up more than twenty-three hours of an executive's week.[55] Imagine how much more it must be now! My clients mention they often spend six hours a day in meetings. These meetings, which are often used to discuss project status, consume precious time that could be used for deep, focused, strategic work. Over 70 percent of senior managers say that meetings are inefficient and unproductive and 64 percent claim that meetings come at the expense of deep thinking.[56] What typically happens in status meetings is participants check email, daydream and write grocery lists while their colleagues drone on about the minutiae of their projects.

If status meetings are needed, they should be short stand-up meetings or huddles. Ideally, status meetings should be replaced with active meetings that aim to:

- Solve a problem.
- Brainstorm a new solution.
- Teach something.
- Create something.
- Have members coach one another (after you teach them how).

As Saeeda learned about each person's style, she continued to nurture an open environment that made it comfortable for the indirect communicators to speak up. The members who had direct styles started speaking their truth in ways that showed more understanding for the need for harmony. They also learned that some of them were open to change while others needed evidence, a forecast of the return on investment and then more proof. Understanding each other's communication styles helped them to be less judgmental and to assume best intentions. Building on this knowledge, Saeeda created space in her meetings so members could share their concerns. Each person was encouraged to express their excitement, reservations and cautions. Rey was kept apprised of the team's work and consulted for big decisions.

I also worked with the team on ways to speak their truth with kindness. When we can formulate our thoughts on what we have observed, how it has

....

55. Steven G. Rogelberg, Cliff Scott and John Kello, "The Science and Fiction of Meetings," *MIT Sloan Management Review* 48, no. 2. (2007).
56. Leslie A. Perlow, and Eunice Eun, "Stop the Meeting Madness," *Harvard Business Review*, From the Magazine (July–August 2017), https://hbr.org/2017/07/stop-the-meeting-madness.

impacted us and what we need from the other, we can slowly start taking risks to speak up. I believe that when we bring together the best of both worlds—direct communicators' need for speaking up and indirect communicators' need for harmony—we have a formula for success.

One of the critical things I shared with the team was the importance of all members standing by one another once they'd made a decision together. Saeeda appreciated this and diligently ensured that the team had time to process and debate through the issues until they came to a solution that worked for a majority of them. I emphasized that sometimes employees will try to sway a manager away from a given initiative or new direction. "Even if you do not love the direction the group has developed, after expressing your opinions, cautions, or dissent, you must agree to get on board and share the same message. No matter how much employees may say negative things about the effort or try to get a different response, you need to stick with the plan." They agreed to this and followed through. Saeeda reported fewer misunderstandings and a decreased feeling of silos.

The team made guidelines for how they would work together and speak up. They also agreed that they would refer back to the steps of the WALK IT model to ensure they were consistently on track with all the steps and on the same wavelength with each other as they kept up with existing projects and took on new initiatives. Saeeda, as the team leader, provided them with feedback.

At one of our final sessions, eight months later, Saeeda strolled in, relaxed and smiling. She shared her team's successes. "Well, I have to say that it took some time, patience and perseverance, but, man, I did it! We did it! We've learned to trust each other and we seek out feedback on our initiatives. We aren't afraid of other members bringing change forward, because we know it will result in a stronger outcome. Of course, we do have some heated moments now and then, but we acknowledge it and power through."

When company leaders are not given the time and space to process issues, brainstorm, problem-solve, or get creative, they eventually learn to stick to their own business and department. Silos are one of the most complex problems for organizations to address. Silos encourage employees to hoard information and assume the worst of others. This attitude hurts collaboration, customer service and team morale. When working on realigning a team, start by seeking their input, making it safe to speak up, making a commitment to stand by one another and following a change methodology such as the WALK IT model. To see if your team is on the same page, you can download the WALK IT survey (and more) from www.apowerfulculture.com.

Ask Yourself

- Do I give my team a chance to share their concerns, ideas, warnings?
- When we come to an agreement, are we united in the message we share with others, or do I later learn that a team member went behind everyone's back with a different message?
- Do we go forward with courage and positive intent to share information and collaborate with other departments so we can break a silo mentality?
- Do I share the steps of change with my team and seek their input?
- Do I hold meetings solely for the purpose of achieving something such as introducing new ideas, problem-solving, group coaching, learning, etc.?

STOP AND START	
⏹ **Stop**	Assuming everyone is on the same page when you give directions.
▶ **Start**	Seeking input, sharing the importance of the change and how each person can live it and drive it.
⏹ **Stop**	Protecting your information from other departments, assuming they will use it against you.
▶ **Start**	Seeing team communication through a lens of positive intent and sharing information and seeking input from your counterparts in other departments.
⏹ **Stop**	Running "efficient" status meetings just so you can check the box.
▶ **Start**	Planning for meetings where you seek input, get aligned and make plans together. Use meeting times for problem-solving, brainstorming, or group learning.

TABLE 11. Align Your Senior Team Checklist

Please note if you take the following actions consistently	YES	NO
I have established a senior team and we guide the organization together.	☐	☐
We can respectfully speak our truths.	☐	☐
Employees will get the same answers from each of us on initiatives or when we drive change.	☐	☐
Points to Consider • What could working on this step do for your culture? How could you apply this to immediate and long-term needs in the areas of innovation and company growth? • What potential action steps should you take? **Suggestions** • Determine who should be on your senior team to help make decisions and drive change. • Read up on facilitation. If needed, seek a trained neutral party to facilitate your sessions.		

Look at Your Culture

The WATCH IT model is about paying attention to your entire culture; observing language, behaviors, dynamics, who is speaking, what is present, what is absent and what is possible. It's about paying attention to your culture from a macro lens. In the WALK IT model, looking at your culture is about looking at your team from a micro lens. It's becoming aware of the specific interactions between managers and employees and employees and customers. It's seeing what actions assist your customers in staying and what actions aid your employees to choose to continue working with you. It's also about encouraging the development of Culture Guardians, employees who care about the culture and will tell you when they see something wrong. If strategy is the what, culture is the how. Culture Guardians are keenly tuned in to the how, to make sure it's going well.

Jane was the VP of Operations at a food manufacturing organization that was growing rapidly through acquisitions. She strode into the meeting room, confident and poised. She was tall and graceful and looked like a model for a women's professional fashion line with her wine-colored sweater; perfectly creased black slacks; dark, wavy shoulder-length hair in place; and a serene, glowing complexion. She was bright, quick and energetic. She possessed a thirst for knowledge and was ready to put in the work. She was engaged in our coaching session and it showed.

Jane had informed me previously that her parent organization had bought six locations around the U.S. These were food companies that had been operating fairly well under mostly family-owned management. The parent company's culture was successful. There were long-term employees who were committed to the company. The company took care of them and they took care of the company. Jane wanted to bring the awesome mindsets and behaviors of the parent company to these new locations but was not quite sure how to do that or how to check on or gauge the health of the culture in the new locations. She asked, "Is culture important enough for me to train my managers on it? How would I do that and how would they ensure that we're creating and sustaining a vibrant culture?"

"All great questions," I said, impressed with Jane's concise and deliberate questions. "What makes this important to you?"

"I want the employees of these six new locations to know they are part of our team, that they belong to something bigger and that they have support. I want to listen to their ideas and not just jam who we are down their throats. I want to operate as one entity, not a group of independent locations. If there is clarity in who we are and what we're doing, I think people will be more motivated and that will also impact our bottom line."

"What would happen if you permitted them to operate independently?"

"We wouldn't get the most out of each location or learn best practices that can be applied across the organization. We would miss out on so much. I already have people from each location giving me advice and sharing their concerns. I've got to bring this together somehow."

Wanting to start with the big picture, I shared the focal point: "If strategy is the what, culture is the how. Culture is how people work together, make decisions, treat each other, treat customers and get results—basically, how things are done. You must keep a finger on the pulse of your culture to ensure its health. A culture is a living organism, because it's made up of people. And it needs regular check-ups."

If Strategy is the What, Culture is the How

If you are growing through acquisitions or opening new locations, integrating the best of your culture will help your company form its identity and grow faster and more efficiently. To replicate or transfer your culture, you will need a plan, people (high-performing Culture Guardians across locations) and ways to measure your outcomes. Clarity on your values is critical as you share and live them throughout your locations. Learning successful ways of doing things will make your new employees feel comfortable.

"Wow!" Jane said. "I like that! So, does that mean that ensuring that people perform the work properly and in a timely manner isn't enough?"

"Yes, exactly. What else is coming to you?" I asked, knowing that her years of experience would provide some insightful perspectives.

"Well, since you mention the 'how,' it's got me thinking about two of my team members. I'm wondering if I've been dismissive of Sato and Rupi."

"Tell me more. Why do you think that is?"

"Well, two people left following our latest acquisition. Sato told me some team members were upset. Rupi mentioned that a few employees said they wanted to better understand the direction of the company. I thought that they were just worrywarts or complainers. Now I'm starting to question that."

I pointed out to Jane that Sato and Rupi sounded like great assets to the company, engaged and committed enough to share their concerns about people's feelings, frustrations and motivations. These types of employees are Culture Guardians.

"Wait, so you're telling me that they're helping me keep a finger on the pulse of our culture?"

"Yes, Jane, they are. They really care. And if you hear them out and take some actions, you'll encourage and empower them to continue caring and spreading this behavior of listening to employee concerns. Remember, you're encouraging them to listen, to care about the culture and to come to you with potential solutions. Otherwise, it may turn into a gossipy type of culture, and you don't want that."

"What else should I do to support them and improve our culture? How can I recruit more Culture Guardians?"

"Great questions! That's why we're here. Before you can train current and future Culture Guardians to scan, correct, grow and sustain your culture, you need to be clear on what's working well, what can improve and the type of culture you generally want. Ask yourself and a sample of formal and informal leaders: What works about your culture? What's going well and what evidence or stories can you share about this? This form of AI[57] helps tap into the best parts of the organization. Ask: When could things have been handled better and what are some habits that can be improved? Listen, take notes and look for the main themes that have emerged.

"Peruse the Glassdoor[58] website. Look for reviews on your company, your competitors and others in your industry. Review the trends among the best and worst companies to work for. What best practices would you like to emulate? What behaviors and mindsets from leaders negatively impact organizations?"

How to Develop Culture Guardians
- Seek their feedback and listen.
- Take their ideas seriously.
- Empower them to help drive your culture.
- Appreciate them.

Jane and I met again three weeks later. "I've learned some amazing things about how much people care about our company," she updated me. "There are themes from the stories about the company's start fifteen years ago until today. The original owner and now his son have driven similar behaviors and attitudes toward customers. They are also both considerate of employees and their families and this shows up in their benefits and

57.   Stavros, Godwin and Cooperrider, Appreciative Inquiry.
58.   Glassdoor, https://www.glassdoor.com.

family-focused gatherings. I would never have known these stories unless I'd asked."

"Great! What else did you learn?" I asked.

"The CEO typically handles the human side of transition well. In the past, he has met with groups of employees to explain any new direction and the rationale. I heard that he's shown empathy for people's emotions while gently explaining the reasons for the change."

"It looks like Sato and Rupi are on to something. They seem to be noticing that the company's best practices have not yet been integrated into the new locations. What did you learn about the areas to work on?"

"Most employees I spoke with said they want to have more clarity on the company's direction and strategy. It will help them make sense of the acquisitions and understand how to keep the company's core culture as we continue to expand."

I was pleased about her progress and enthusiasm and how she was putting everything together. I leaned back in my seat and smiled. This is what it's all about, I thought to myself. "Love it, Jane! What else?"

"The Glassdoor reviews are enlightening. I mean, I take it with a grain of salt, because I know that it's likely the happiest and most angry people who take the time to write reviews. That being said, the trends are clear. The top companies have leaders who give clear direction and create an environment where people feel valued beyond salary. The lowest rated companies seem to have high turnover and have a strong focus on profits over people. There are mentions of uncomfortable working conditions, long hours and little work-life balance. The people side of those businesses are suffering. How many Culture Guardians were they listening to? Or did they even have any? If they did, maybe they would have helped to sniff out trouble, like those detection dogs at the airport!"

"I like the metaphor of sniffing out trouble. That's creative," I said before asking if she wanted more resources.

"Yes, please, I'm ready!" Jane exclaimed.

I shared other practices for sniffing out not just trouble, but also good ideas, concerns and suggestions as a way of evaluating culture:

For Your Overall Culture: Get curious, get out of your office and start talking to people. "Just walk around aimlessly?" you may ask. Not exactly. Getting curious means taking the time to find out how people are doing and what they're working on. "But we know what they're working on during our meetings and Zooms." For sure.—*And* there's something unique about casually dropping by for conversations. "Well, how often would make sense? I don't want this to be awkward." I get it. For some people, it's twice a week in the afternoon. Ask people how they are doing, how work is going and what observations they've made. Keep it casual. Sometimes it will just be chitchat about kids, weekends, travel and sports. That's okay. This is about relationship-building. The ideas and feedback will come. In my research on San Diego's fastest growing companies,[59] each of the eight CEOs I interviewed shared that they walked around and spoke with employees regularly. Culture surveys are another way of getting an overall impression of how people are doing. Online surveys can certainly give a snapshot of the culture, but they can also have some downsides, including often not being completely anonymous and not getting the depth of information you would via a qualitative culture survey from a third party.

For Your Teams: Conduct skip-level meetings where the CEO or a higher-up manager meets with employees who are more than one step down the chain of command. Use the time to educate people on the strategy (see Know Your Plan, p.184). Make sure to seek input and suggestions.

For Individuals: Become familiar with and use Gallup's Q^{12} Employee Engagement Survey.[60] Conduct "stay interviews" that ask your employees why they choose to stay with the company and what they value.

....

59.   Shahrzad Sherry Nooravi, PsyD, published research on eight of the top twenty CEOs of San Diego's Fastest Growing Companies, as identified by the *San Diego Business Journal,* 2012.

60.   Gallup, *Q12 Employee Engagement Survey.*

Ask Yourself

- Do I put off asking for feedback because I'm afraid of what I will learn?
- How can I prepare myself and my ego to be open to constructive suggestions?
- Can I create new ways of being that are based on my values around health, sports, giving back, lifelong learning, etc., that would get the team excited?
- Can I conduct Stay Interviews with some of my best performers to learn what makes them stay and what else we can be doing to motivate our teams?

STOP AND START	
Stop	Assuming everything is fine just because your employees tell you so.
Start	Handling your ego, releasing what your ego might be telling you, put on some "armor" to toughen up and regularly ask formal and informal leaders across the company what they really think about the culture.
Stop	Creating external "fixes" like putting in coffee machines and Ping-Pong tables to engage people, because you've seen other companies doing this.
Start	Having confidence that you can shape the culture you want.
Stop	Blaming your "lazy," "unmotivated," "bland" culture on your people.
Start	Investigating what you may be doing that is driving this behavior and take accountability for the power that you have to change things. Good news: you can change culture from the inside out by focusing on you. In the process of doing so, you will drive more of who you are and what you want.

TABLE 12. Look at Your Culture Checklist

Please note if you take the following actions consistently	YES	NO
Our team members demonstrate high energy and a sense of ownership through their behaviors.	☐	☐
We actively communicate, demonstrate and reinforce our cultural priorities.	☐	☐
We have identified the areas of our culture that are hurting our organization.	☐	☐

Points to Consider

- What potential action steps should you take?
- What could working on this step do for your culture?

Suggestions

- Seek feedback from your staff on what is and isn't working in the culture. (Do this only if you can commit to following up with findings and making some changes.)
- Conduct "stay" interviews to understand why people want to stay with your company. Ask questions like:
  - What do you look forward to when you come to work each day?
  - What do you like most or least about working here?
  - What would make your job more satisfying?
  - How do you like to be recognized?
  - What talents are not being used in your current role?

Know Your Plan

Where are you going? How will you get there?

More often than you might expect, employees cannot articulate the company's strategy when asked. Typically, the strategy is developed by the senior team at a two-day retreat. Binders of the plan are distributed but rarely referred to. Some leaders can remember a couple of the items, but clarity is lacking.

Imagine what it would be like to have a clear one-page strategy where every employee—from the administrative staff to the manufacturing plant and everyone in between—is able to articulate the top three to five things the company seeks to accomplish. There would be different conversations, different questions, less confusion and likely better outcomes.

Luis came into the conference room, bright-eyed in his plaid shirt and medium-blue distressed jeans. "I've had my coffee and I'm ready to go!" He was the VP of sales for a clothing manufacturer, responsible for developing business to business opportunities for distributing the company's creations to retailers. After ten years of success creating fashion for big retailers, the company was looking to expand.

The problem was that no one was clear on the how and it was affecting Luis and his sales team as they reached out to retailers. "When we can't speak clearly on what we want to do and how, we look ill-prepared and I think this makes potential partners not want to work with us." He shared that he had observed several of his sales managers in meetings with distributors. "To be honest, they were not inspirational. There was no clear plan." Leaders could not articulate the company's vision or strategy and Luis was concerned that this sent an unclear message to the larger business community. It was also difficult to stay focused. People would follow different leads or ideas without vetting them with the rest of the group or knowing if they fit into the overall strategy. "We're kind of all over the place, taking meetings with anyone, just grasping at anything we can get our hands on."

"How would you like things to be?" I asked, curious about how he could get everyone on the same page. It was clear that the current situation was already impacting business.

"We've talked about new partnerships, creating more than women's tops and bottoms; maybe creating different pieces and expanding through opening a new plant; maybe having a couple of acquisitions. But we haven't made any progress."

He shared that the senior team had created a strategy six months ago at an off-site retreat. When I asked him for it, he chuckled and took a spiral book out of his brown leather crossbody bag.

As I thumbed through it, I asked what he thought about the strategy and how they referred to this information.

"I think we were well-intentioned when we assembled this. There are good things in there. We don't really use it as intended, though. We'll pull it out from time to time, but it's not really a living document that we follow."

Not surprised, I asked if the middle managers, supervisors and frontline workers knew the strategy and where they should focus their efforts, outside of fulfilling existing orders.

"Yeah, right. That would be ideal. I don't even know how we would do that and what we should expect from that. Strategic plans are hard enough to understand as they are. It would be great to get ideas and feedback from all our staff. Another factor is, how would our mostly Spanish-speaking frontline workers understand this and what would be the purpose?"

"You're asking all the right questions, Luis! The most ideal situation is to have your strategy on one page, clear and concise for everyone to understand and follow—and to have it available in both Spanish and English. You can get more ideas when people know where you're trying to go. Your frontline staff are the ones touching the fabrics, seeing the patterns, being the eyes and ears on the manufacturing floor. It can only help, right?"

"I never thought about that," Luis answered. "I've always seen long plans that stay at the senior team and manager level. This would be quite a departure from that. Is this a good time for me to share some of the challenges and ask how we'd address it?"

"Yes, let's talk about it and how you can create a clear path for everyone."

"Our sales team will meet with retailers who share their ideas and trends and what their customers are looking for. They'll tell the customers, 'Let me see if we can create this.' And then Juan, the head of operations, takes a look and says the design is too complex or that we're doing fine with what we're already working on. That seems to halt progress."

Luis and I planned for me to facilitate a strategy session with the leadership team to clarify the strategy and get it down to one page. The meeting included reviewing the current state of affairs, challenges and opportunities. We prioritized a long list of actions down to four main actions with a plan and timeline. The vision became "Style, quality and cutting-edge designs for today's modern woman." The strategies focused on decreasing error rates, developing partnerships, creating new clothing lines and building a location in Tijuana. The vision and the strategies were prepared in English and Spanish and distributed throughout the organization.

Across several sessions, Luis shared that by reflecting on the strategies and learning more about employee empowerment, intercultural communication and driving accountability, he had come up with new ways to handle ideas and requests for change. His first response was typically, "Let's refer back to the vision!" and "Does it match our current strategy?" There was a clear plan for where the company was going and how they were going to get there.

He was especially proud of the steps taken to empower frontline employees by giving them a say in the initial options for material and design and encouraging them to speak up to the supervisors if quality was lacking or if they noticed a mistake in the production line. Luis and I had discussed the differences in intercultural communication and how Latin American cultures have a higher power distance[61] (meaning that because of a high level of respect for authority, employees are less likely to speak up to managers about errors or ideas for improvement). Luis brought in coaching for the supervisors to develop growth and openness to seeking feedback and having mistakes pointed out. When you train managers to seek and reward this feedback and you train employees to speak up, you create a great opportunity for driving quality and innovation while decreasing errors.

Your company will make progress when you have a clear, concise plan of the growth strategy and how you will get there. Your company's vision and strategy should be a one-page document (not a large binder that sits on a shelf) that you share with all employees in all relevant languages. Once you have developed this, ask several people to hold you accountable to it, especially if you are a flexible type of leader who thrives on firefighting. (See No More Firefighting: Get Focused, Create Direction and Get Started, p.80) Use the strategy document to help you make decisions on your direction, product and plans for growth.

....

61.   Geert Hofstede, "The 6-D Model of National Culture," accessed October 16, 2021, https://geerthofstede.com/culture-geert-hofstede-gert-jan-hofstede/6d-model-of-national-culture.

Ask Yourself

- If I asked a sample of employees what our top few strategic goals are, would they be able to identify them?
- Do I have a clear, simple vision that everyone can articulate? If not, can I partner with some team members to create one?
- What would it take for me to create a one-page strategy document with input from my senior team and key leaders that outlines our vision, values and key strategies for the next three to five years?

STOP AND START	
■ Stop	Assuming your leaders will promote company growth. Not everyone wants to get out of their comfort zone.
▶ Start	Evaluating your strategy every three years, creating the strategy for three to five major areas and how you will guide every department leader to collaborate to achieve the goal.
■ Stop	Creating long strategic plans that no one refers to.
▶ Start	Creating a short, precise strategic plan on one page that can be distributed to employees at all levels in the languages they speak.
■ Stop	Thinking having a vision and values is a nice-to-have exercise but not important for driving culture.
▶ Start	Examining how the most successful companies and their employees are crystal clear on their vision and strategic plan and how they'll get there using their values.

TABLE 13. Know Your Plan Checklist

Please note if you take the following actions consistently	YES	NO
Our teams refer to our vision, strategy and values daily.	☐	☐
We have a plan and process for hiring, onboarding, growing and rewarding talent and coaching them out when necessary.	☐	☐
Our management team is accountable for developing, guiding and coaching team members.	☐	☐

Points to Consider

- What potential action steps should you take?
- What could working on this step do for your culture?

Suggestions

- With support from your strategic HR leader, identify and clarify your vision, strategy and values by facilitating several leadership team sessions. Share your results and receive feedback from your formal and informal leaders.
- Integrate your vision, strategy and values into your performance management program (ideally using software that allows everyone to complete evaluations online—including self-evaluations).
- Teach your staff how to coach and give feedback. Start with *Whale Done!: The Power of Positive Relationships.*

Integrate Values

Dana greeted me in the pristine white lobby of her company, an architecture firm. Vibrant shades of navy, turquoise and light blue—the colors of the company's logo—were painted vertically behind the front reception desk, a welcome standout amidst the white space. Plaques on the walls displayed the company's support of local and national charities. As the two of us entered through the glass doors past security, I saw many beautiful images of employees and customers in a mix of color, sepia and black-and-white photographs in ornate frames of gold, copper and pewter. As a lover of all things design, I felt a bit giddy encountering all this beauty and took mental notes to share with my family members who appreciate such things. As we rounded the corner, there it was: the almighty list of core values, the behaviors that the company leaders had determined were important for employees and leaders alike to follow. *Collaboration, Openness* and *Customer Service* were some of the words I saw on the list.

Whenever I see a company's core values on the wall, whether in conference rooms or online, I wonder how they're serving the company and if people are living by them. How do people treat one another and customers? How do they speak up, if they speak up? How open are they to change? How are high performers who mistreat others handled? Are the leaders behaving ethically?

From my call with Dana, the HR director, I had a heads-up that the leaders' behaviors were not aligned with the values they espoused. When this happens, people can become demoralized and look elsewhere for work. The cost of recruiting, hiring and training new staff is high, along with the loss of institutional knowledge. I wondered how this company was faring.

Dana's heels clicked on the marble floors as she led me into her office. She was wearing a light blue pantsuit cropped at the ankle, a cream silk blouse and a bold brass African-style necklace. We took a seat across from each other on two couches, one turquoise and one navy. I admired the surrounding aesthetic and appreciated the harmony and consistency of the design throughout the space.

Organizing and Communicating your Plan for Success

- **Vision:** The company vision outlines the desired future position of the company and what the organization wants to become. It is ideally short and memorable.

- **Mission:** The mission focuses on today and includes what the company does, who it serves and how it serves them.

- **Strategy:** The company strategy is a long-term plan that includes the type of products/services that you plan to build and the customers and markets you want to sell to.

- **Values:** The core values are the fundamental beliefs of an organization that help guide behavior. Values can be used for decision-making, recruiting and promoting and rewarding the right behaviors.

- **Goals:** These are what a company expects to accomplish over a specific period of time. Businesses usually outline their goals and objectives in their business plans. Goals might pertain to the company as a whole, departments, employees, customers, or any other area of the business.

What Are Core Values and Why Should I Use Them?

Core values are the beliefs of an organization about how people should behave. These values can be a guide to making decisions and determining if employees are behaving according to the company's standards. These standards are typically centered around how staff should work with one another and customers.

You can also create your own personal core values for yourself and your family. The more a person's core values are similar to a company's core values, the more of a fit there will be and the more successful the person will be in that organization.

Dana was savvy and direct. "As you know, I want to speak with you about changes we've had, including a new principal and an updated strategy. We're asking employees to come up with new ideas and shift their thinking to meet our customers' needs. I just don't know how we're going to get our people there. Employees are clear on the strategy and are doing their best to contribute, but something is not clicking and I sense that people are discouraged. They're great employees and I don't want to lose them. I think the style of the new principal partner may be part of the problem. Employees come into my office frustrated and say that they feel punished when they try to give new ideas or are shut down quickly when they try to be innovative. They don't feel heard. It's not a good situation. I've had five high-performing employees state that this is not the company they know and that it no longer feels collaborative. Our company needs to get aligned on our core values or we will lose good people and their ideas." She sighed and slumped a bit on the sofa.

Although Dana looked perfectly put together with beautiful shoulder-length ringlet curls and daytime chic burgundy lips, her body language said something else. She had worked for other large companies and knew how values should be integrated into a company. I suspected that she did not know how to sell the importance of this to her senior team.

"Another issue is the values are dated," Dana continued. "They were developed maybe ten years ago. They feel a bit generic and not specific to the big things we are trying to do. Collaboration, openness and customer service are nice, but not enough. Our new three-year plan requires a lot of innovation and our being disrupters in our industry. It's going to require new behaviors. I wonder about updating the values to include innovation, courage and even empathy.

However, I'm not sure if working on the values is the executive team's top priority—plus it looks like a lot of work!" she said, exasperated.

I asked Dana to share more about why she thought updating the values was important.

"Well, the right core values help shape the culture and help identify the best behaviors that bring success, right?"

I agreed and shared other benefits of having core values. Establishing strong core values provides both internal and external value. Think of core values as the beliefs, philosophies and best behaviors that have brought and will bring success to the company. Internally, they can be used for decision-making and for recruiting and promoting people as well as exiting someone from the company. Externally, core values tell the world who your company is, what your company believes and how you operate. This is increasingly important to job seekers. They want to work somewhere that is clear and consistent about how it does business.

Core Values Shape Company Culture

Once you have identified your core values, you can use them for:

- **Recruiting:** Ask interview questions around the behaviors that are important to you. If you use behavioral interviewing techniques, you will get real examples that will help you know if a candidate possesses the mindset and behaviors you seek.
- **Promotions:** Does this person live and promote these values? Can he or she be a role model for others?
- **Exit:** Have you coached this person toward the values with little success? Perhaps the company is no longer a fit and the person's behavior does not promote what you are building.

Dana said that as much as she liked the concept of core values, she had not seen core values fully lived at any of the companies she had worked for so far. "Do employees really care about words on a wall? I don't want to go through a big exercise of helping the company identify their values if the leaders are not going to follow them."

"That's fair and I appreciate your honesty, Dana. Here are some things to know about the human psyche. To a degree, structure and consistency make us comfortable, because we know what we can expect. Included in this are guidelines and boundaries for behavior. This goes for everyone in the company, regardless of division or position. Everyone should be living to these values. You may also need to add new values to reflect the updated strategy. For example, I saw that driving new business and tapping into new markets is a big focus of your new strategy. So your instinct to add innovation and courage as part of the update may be right on."

With her energy building, Dana sat straight up. "Yes! Okay, I'm seeing this. Will you help us articulate our values?"

One month later, I facilitated a meeting with the company's executives and helped them identify potential values in our first session. Following are some of the questions I asked the group:

- What great behaviors got your company here?
- What is your philosophy for how people should work together?
- How important is it for your team to share their ideas?
- How will you become disrupters in your space?
- What is your view on innovation?
- How do you want to treat your customers?
- What are new ways of looking at customer care based on the changing market and evolving customer preferences?
- Are there new behaviors the company needs to cultivate to realize the updated strategy?

The first draft the group came up with contained seven values. The team felt so excited to have their thoughts on paper. I congratulated them for their hard work and encouraged them to see if they could collapse the values down to four or five items. We refined them again until they were near perfect. All the employees were asked to give their input so that they had some familiarity with the values by the time they were published. I facilitated learning sessions for employees on how they could live these values. At least two of the senior team members participated actively in these sessions and shared examples for how they would like to see the new values activated.

At a coaching session three months later, Dana was positive and shared that she and the rest of the executives were using the updated core values in creative ways. One was reinforcing the behaviors of innovation, courage and inclusion. They started giving kudos and appreciation to staff for living the values at the company meetings. When they had to change how they were approaching client issues and someone said, "We've always done it that way and it has worked," they would refer to the value of innovation. Two employees started sharing new ideas at staff meetings and later asked, "Am I living our core values in a better way? We're trying to be more curious and open to change." Several employees who tended to complain about others started being more open and less accusatory when asked, "What positive intention can you see behind your colleagues' behavior?" Other employees came up with new ways to celebrate holidays by scheduling relevant presentations. These included bringing in an organization that supported veterans to speak before Veterans Day and a diversity, equity and inclusion trainer present before Martin Luther King Jr. Day.

Dana and I also planned for how she would create behavioral interviewing[62] questions for determining if a candidate was a good fit. She created guidelines to use during performance review meetings so the company could better measure how employees were performing their work. We also discussed how employees could start sharing the company's values with customers.

Your company's core values can be considered the heartbeat of your organization. It's the essence of how the work is done, how teams collaborate and how customers are treated. These values can be an internal compass for making important decisions and behaving consistently. Developing the values can be guided by the senior team reviewing how the company has become successful and what else the company needs to reach success. Core values must be reviewed every several years to determine if they are relevant given evolving technology, industry changes and changing customer preferences. Values can be used externally to share with the world who you are and how you operate. This is critical for job seekers who want to be part of a thriving culture with clear values that guide behavior.

....

62. Behavioral interviewing is a technique for interviewing candidates to determine if they have demonstrated the behavior you want to hire for. For example, if you are seeking candidates who are innovative, you can ask a question like, "Please describe a time when you tried an innovative approach to solving a problem." Behavioral interviewing creates an opportunity for candidates to describe real-life examples that demonstrate the behavior you are seeking.

Ask Yourself

- Have we articulated the core values and behaviors that make us successful? Do they include behaviors we need to meet our future strategic goals? If so, when was the last time they were updated? (Make sure you revisit them every three to five years.) Are they short, simple and to the point?
- How can we live by our core values and operate our business using the core values?
- How can we integrate coaching conversations that incorporate our core values and the behaviors we want to live by?
- Are our core values clear enough that if an employee was misaligned with them, others would advise the senior team to take actions?

STOP AND START	
■ **Stop**	Showcasing your values online and/or throughout your office only.
▶ **Start**	Making decisions based on the core values and articulating to others when you've done so.
■ **Stop**	Thinking core values are a nice-to-have set of behaviors.
▶ **Start**	Learning how the most successful companies have very clear core values by which they live and work.
■ **Stop**	Reviewing your employees' performance based solely on their job metrics.
▶ **Start**	Incorporating your core values into performance reviews so you are measuring not just the what (metrics), but also the how of your employees working together, treating customers well and demonstrating the specific behaviors that are important for your company.
■ **Stop**	Believing that only HR can be a coach to employees.
▶ **Start**	Teaching coaching skills to your team leads so they can coach one another as well as employees on the values and strategy.

TABLE 14. Integrate Your Values Checklist

Please note if you take the following actions consistently	YES	NO
We have shared our values with our teams and they refer to the values regularly and live up to them at work.	☐	☐
We hire to the values we have identified and embraced.	☐	☐
When we need to make firing decisions, we refer to our values.	☐	☐

Points to Consider

- What potential action steps should you take?
- What could working on this step do for your culture?

Suggestions

- Write down some of the behaviors and guiding values that have brought success to your team. As you look forward to your future strategy, ask yourself what new behaviors need to be on this list.
- Meet with your HR leader and discuss how you can incorporate the values into hiring, development and offboarding.
- If you have created values, review them and honestly consider if they are still relevant or if they need to be refreshed.

Track Everything

Randalyn was a regional manager at a construction company that was growing quickly through acquiring smaller companies across the U.S. She walked into the conference room wearing perfectly creased khaki pants, hiking shoes and an olive polo shirt with the company logo on the top right pocket. She was tall, slim and no-nonsense. I noticed a bit of dried mud on her shoes and wondered if she had just returned from a job site. She extended her hand and gave me a firm, brisk handshake.

Appreciating her strong and straightforward style, I sat back down and asked her where she would like to begin. After taking a long sip from her water bottle, she took a deep breath and exclaimed, "We are growing! Our company is making moves and things are going well overall. I just came back from one of our acquisitions and had a big realization: We need to ingrain our culture at each of these sites. Yes, these people are good; however, I want them to operate and make decisions as we do. To treat their team with respect. To put customers first. These are important values that have brought us success. I came here out of college and have had the best experience growing within the firm, so I should know. But we were smaller then and we need to formalize our processes now that we have fifteen locations. We need to spread our culture."

As we spoke, it became clear that to ensure strong management at each of these new sites, Randalyn would need to fast-track the development of her current account managers so that they would be ready to become branch managers at the new locations. I agreed with her that sharing the positive leadership of her staff would drive a strong and consistent culture. She had the support of Adab, the CEO, and Jesús, the COO, to develop a system to grow their people. They were on the same page regarding talent management, including clarity on job expectations, values and goals. Managers would need to learn how to give regular feedback and employees would learn how to drive their own careers and evaluate their own performance honestly. It was clear that creating a talent management system would support the growing company having shared leadership behaviors across their locations versus "islands" where locations operated differently.

Randalyn faced a challenge when she began talking about the importance of giving regular feedback and creating a performance review system to track accountability and measure employees' performance to the company's goals. She was up against a feedback-shy culture. "We need to be careful on this," Adab and Jesús told her. "We've never given formal feedback and people may be intimidated and not understand why we are doing it."

Time for transformation! Creating an accountability system and tracking performance is not easy, but it is key to growing your people and company. The final part of the WALK IT model is about tracking the measurables of the plan you have created (Know Your Plan). You achieve what you pay attention to and you get what you measure, as challenging as it may be.

In this case, the company plan was to know who their talent was, what they needed to grow and what progress they were making. I helped the company develop their system in the months that followed, with Randalyn and other regional managers in the role of boots on the ground, pushing the effort forward.

Six weeks later when we met, Randalyn seemed annoyed. "The employees are uncomfortable with the idea of tracking performance. Some have asked, 'Is this so it will be easier to get rid of some of us? Are we having layoffs? Why do we need to do this now? We've never done it in our thirty-year history.' Can you believe it?" she asked as she ran her hand through her short blond hair.

Her own experience, she said, as she had worked her way up from a super-intendent to account manager to branch manager to regional manager, was to seek feedback regularly in every position so she could grow. She was bothered that she was facing so much resistance. I was not surprised in the least about the employees' concerns. The company had been around for more than three decades, operating successfully without having formal performance reviews. At the end of each year, staff would hear a "Good job!" and receive a modest raise. That was it. They may have been confused as to why it was important to have performance reviews now. Randalyn needed to explain the why and the team needed to learn the how to get this change off the ground.

"Share with me what you make of this," I said to Randalyn.

"Well, I guess I could understand why they are wondering about this. We've gotten this far without it. Perhaps they're scared."

"Tell me more."

"If I put myself in their shoes, I could see how they would be fearful for their jobs. I never had that outlook. I was always pushing and seeking feedback, even if it hurt. I was taught by my parents to be tough and learn how to be my best. I've been checking in with my teachers since grade school to learn how to get As and what I could do to improve if I did not ace the exam."

"Wow," was all I could say. She was a unique and talented person who didn't shy away from criticism. If she could bottle up and sell this verve and for-titude, she'd be set for life.

"I'm starting to think that perhaps I'm judging people by my standards, comparing them to who I am. Just talking to you about my background makes me realize this."

I continued working with the executive team and Randalyn, as the operational point of contact, to create a sustainable system. She led the company to understand that one of the most important practices that helps an organization to "get organized" is creating accountability systems. It's great to say, "We need to grow the company this year," but the question is how and by how much and by when? What are the concrete goals each person needs to accomplish to get you there? Want to know how your sales team did compared to this time last year? Check your measurements. How are each of your departments performing toward their goals? Let's check on those results. Are they easy to measure? Are they SMART goals?[63] How many high performers in the organization are ready to be promoted to the next position? Check your talent management plan.

The majority of Fortune 500 companies have systems for measuring how each employee, team and department is progressing toward company goals. These systems are typically sophisticated and measure progress on goals as well as on specific competencies[64] or behaviors for each role. At times, these programs can be a bit long, but they work well and feed into the company's talent management system.[65] They help clarify how each person is progressing, whether as a high performer, good performer, or someone who needs further development in their role and/or competencies. The system should also measure how each person is living the company's values (see Integrate Values, p.189).

Once an organization begins to gain clarity on its vision, mission, strategy, values and goals, it begins moving toward its goals with more ease and confidence. People don't scratch their heads, wondering what's most important for their role. They have clarity on decision-making, because they have guiding principles and values.

---

63. A SMART goal is a goal that is Specific, Measurable, Achievable, Results-focused and Time-bound. A SMART goal enables you to check progress and determine if a particular goal has been completed or not.

64. A competency is a group of knowledge and skills that enables a person to perform effectively in a job or situation. Competencies refer to the how of a person's abilities.

65. The purpose of a talent management system is to ensure that there are enough high-performing workers (talent) to help meet a company's business objectives. One of the key objectives of human resources is to create a strategic workforce by recruiting the right talent and developing and growing them in the organization. When done right, the organization will retain high performers longer.

It doesn't stop there, though. You can have the best system for tracking performance and a strong human resource leader supporting the effort, but that doesn't automatically mean that performance gets tracked. I shared with Randalyn some research from HBR showing that the single most shirked responsibility of executives is holding people accountable.[66] In HBR's survey of more than five thousand upper-level managers from the US, Europe, Latin America and Asia-Pacific, 46 percent of respondents rated "too little" on the item, "Holds people accountable—firm when they don't deliver."[67] Remarkably, the results holds up no matter how you slice the data, whether by ratings from bosses, peers, or even subordinates. There could be several explanations for this finding:

- Some leaders focus on maintaining harmony and don't like to be seen as the "bad guy" who gives the bad news. (See False Harmony Gets You Nowhere: Embrace Conflict and Liberate the Truth, p.59)
- Some leaders are flexible types and have a hard time sticking to a regimented plan of giving regular feedback. (See No More Firefighting: Get Focused, Create Direction and Get Started, p.80)
- There is a movement toward working on people's strengths versus weaknesses. Tom Rath's book *StrengthsFinder 2.0*[68] and the Gallup Organization's emphasis on how organizations can thrive by helping employees work toward their areas of strength has been a big hit as organizations seek to make better matches with people's natural abilities and job responsibilities.
- Many millennials have grown up in environments where they've received regular praise and recognition for their efforts. Fast-forward to the work environment and they expect their managers to notice their work and can be "indignant when feedback is not forthcoming." According to HBR, they are not particularly open to critical feedback: "...at a time when talent retention and engaging employees is *de rigueur*," management may get advice to not "give employees a hard time about their weaknesses, celebrate their strengths."[69]

66. Darren Overfield and Rob Kaiser, "One out of Every Two Managers Is Terrible at Accountability," *Harvard Business Review,* November 8, 2012, https://hbr.org/2012/11/one-out-of-every-two-managers-is-terrible-at-accountability.
67. Overfield and Kaiser, Managers Terrible at Accountability.
68. Tom Rath, *StrengthsFinder 2.0* (Gallup Press, 2007).
69. Overfield and Kaiser, Managers Terrible at Accountability.

Randalyn sat back in her chair, seemingly frustrated by this information. "I think I have enough challenges just getting this program started and now I learn that managers neglect giving real feedback? Doesn't that create average performance when leaders are too scared to give the real feedback?"

"It can. I believe it is important to share positive feedback on what the employee is doing well. It often helps to then ask the employee what they think could be better. You'd be surprised how aware they can be. Then share your thoughts on what can be done better next time and brainstorm on future actions. Otherwise, you may have a mediocre team, just getting by."

I shared another concept with Randalyn. "You can also get employees to coach one another by creating a coaching culture where you train your leaders on coaching best practices and incorporate their doing so as part of their job requirements. A simple first step is to teach employees to 'feedforward.'[70] The idea is that once a person has a goal in mind, they describe the goal to a colleague, friend or family member and ask for two suggestions for achieving the goal; they respond to the suggestions with 'thank you' only."

Randalyn and her team and I continued to collaborate to support employees' understanding the importance of feedback, goals and performance management through the following steps:

- The managers learned how to give positive and corrective feedback as well as how to write a performance review with constructive suggestions and goals that were reviewed each quarter.
- Employees learned how to assess their own performance so they could write a balanced self-evaluation. They rated themselves on a 4-point scale, where 1 meant Needs Improvement and 4 meant Outstanding. Many people assessing their performance for the first time gave themselves all 4s until they were coached on how to use the scale.
- I helped Randalyn and the other regional managers and some account managers develop competencies for each position.
- In training sessions, leaders shared what it would look like to live the organization's values.

....

70. Feedforward is a term coined by Marshall Goldsmith in *What Got You Here Won't Get You There* (Hyperion, 2007).

Four months later, Randalyn updated me that employees were happy with the program. They liked getting feedback and realized it was something they were missing. Seeing how to create and work toward SMART goals was another area they were happy about. One employee had told her, "I thought this was punitive at first, but it's actually the opposite and we get to grow in our roles."

Some of the branch managers complained about having to write more than eight performance reviews. Randalyn coached them on what a difference it makes to individuals, the team and the company to receive feedback. I encouraged her to take these managers out for a special meal to celebrate their efforts.

Two months after that, Randalyn was able to promote five account managers to branch managers. After identifying their strong performance and desire to grow, she had them job-shadow other branch managers and have executive coaching so they could improve their management skills. Randalyn was pleased with her results and also started informally seeking feedback from customers.

Creating an accountability system and tracking performance is not easy, but it is key to growing your people and company. The goals you measure will flow from your vision, mission and strategic plan. It is critical to include job responsibilities and values (the how) in your measurement system. Transforming vague goals into SMART goals will ensure that each person is clear on what they need to be working on at all times. Employees need to understand why you are creating a performance review system and how it will help them. They also need to give input on their own performance by writing self-evaluations.

According to research, giving constructive feedback is one of the least favorite parts of a manager's job, but it's vital to focus on strengths, seek feedback from the employees and share your suggestions for how to improve future performance. A strong system will ensure you are developing your people to align with future company growth. Strong performers will also tend to stay at companies that develop their skills. Implementing great plans and achieving great goals hinge on great measurement!

Ask Yourself

- Am I willing, perhaps with the support of my HR leader, to ask employees about how often and how well they receive coaching from our leaders?

- Have I provided coach training for our managers so they can most effectively coach their staff? How can we foster a coaching culture?

- Do we have a functional performance management system that allows us to track our talent? Does this system empower employees to write self-assessments to share with their managers? Do we use performance data to plan how to coach and grow our employees?

- Do we seek feedback from our customers on what we are doing well and what else we can be doing to support them?

STOP AND START
Stop Complaining about having to write performance reviews for your people. They need to know how they're doing. If you have discussions each month and track your employees' progress, the annual review should be a summary and hopefully a celebration. Don't save everything for the last minute.
Start Seeing that giving feedback is as necessary as drinking water. It keeps your employees fresh and hydrated.
Stop Running away when you have to give difficult feedback.
Start Tracking performance and giving constructive feedback in a professional and caring manner.
Stop Being afraid of seeking feedback from your customers. They will respect you more for it and you will create customers who keep coming back.
Start Creating a simple system to check in with your customers every three to six months. Ask how things are going, what can be better and what ideas they have for new products or services. You'd be surprised at how much they can help you improve your offerings.

TABLE 15. Track Everything Checklist

Please note if you take the following actions consistently	YES	NO
We track progress toward goals as a company, as departments and as individuals.	☐	☐
We have a clear talent management program; at all times, we know who needs what kind of development.	☐	☐
We provide coach training for our managers.	☐	☐
We regularly seek feedback from customers.	☐	☐
Points to Consider ■ What potential action steps should you take? ■ What could working on this step do for your culture? **Suggestions** ■ Learn about accountability best practices in your industry. ■ Discuss performance and talent management opportunities with your team. ■ Create a simple way for your staff to seek and track feedback from customers.		

Conclusion: Tend to Culture, a Living Organism

Your culture is a living organism with deep-rooted values and behaviors, and when it is nurtured, it will remain healthy and withstand the test of time, changing conditions and the many storms that will come your way. The stronger the roots of culture, the more your company can be resilient during crises and difficult times, through changes in industry, technology, competition, or worldwide challenges such as pandemics. When you tap into and care for the roots of your culture, you create a thriving workplace where people stay longer and give their best.

A Grounded You is a Grounded Culture

In *A Powerful Culture Starts with You*, you may have observed that, as a leader, the culture of your team and company reflects your personality and roots, be that your assumptions about the world, biases, personal style and background (cultural upbringing, views about gender roles, your generation, etc.). Your style impacts your company's style. There's much to celebrate about this, as it informs how you shape culture in the best way. And, if things are not going well, taking a deep dive into your style and background can give you clues as to where your style may have become overplayed or no longer serves you.

You, as the leader, are the most powerful instrument for shaping culture. You have the agency and the ability to be the change you want to see. Do you want your leaders to walk the talk? Ensure you do so. Do you want a certain level of customer service? Model it and train others to create loyal customers. Do you want your team to coach their employees more? Start coaching your leaders. Do you want your leaders to speak their mind and have boundaries? Work up the courage to do the same.

One of the biggest frustrations clients share with me is "Our leader encourages us to do one thing and then turns around and does the opposite." Taking the time to change this will pay off in many ways, including more motivated team members and more of the behaviors you want to see that bring success.

Partnering with a coach and investing in leadership development in general can aid you in exploring what you want to be different in your company or among your leaders. Deep inner work begins with your openness to feedback and suggestions. Any change you want to see is within your reach when you recognize that everything starts with you.

Tools for Tapping into Your Power and Potential

Maximize your Time: Working on your culture will take time plus mental and emotional energy. There are several tools in this book that will help you maximize your time, energy and esteem. It is critical to continually analyze your tasks and meetings. Ask Yourself: What do you no longer need to do and what can others do that will help them grow? What meetings do you need to excuse yourself from? What meetings can you influence to be conducted in a different way?

Find Esteem in Wonderful Places: The Esteem Portfolio is a tool that you can refer to for the purpose of maintenance and, in particular, when your energy is low or when you don't feel the spark that gets you up and going with a positive attitude. When you take time to find joy outside of work—whether in exercise, hobbies, spending time with family, reading, or reflecting—you will show up as a more calm, reflective leader. It will take an investment of your time to do things outside of work, but doing so will support you in becoming a focused, joyful leader with whom it is a pleasure to work.

Embrace the Steps for Continual Growth: WATCH IT, DRIVE IT®, WALK IT®

The three models in this book can be used as your company and leadership grow and face change and adversity. WATCH IT is a tool to observe your culture and is most effective when used on a regular basis, particularly as your company evolves. You may hear employees who have been with the company since the early stages lament that "Things are different now and not like they used to be." Use WATCH IT to grasp the root behaviors and best practices that brought the company here. Ensure that you use these behaviors as you expand and scale. Doing so will create a similar feeling and set of assumptions, beliefs and behaviors in other locations.

DRIVE IT is a coaching tool to use for yourself and with others. It can become a go-to tool for coaching conversations that drive motivation and results. It can also help you shake off your doubts and gain clarity around achieving positive change.

WALK IT ensures that your senior team is on the same page, driving toward the same results. As your company grows and leaders leave or get promoted into senior roles, or you bring in leaders from the outside, the group dynamic changes. It will be critical to use the steps of this model to keep everyone aligned, speaking up and elegantly making decisions that they support together.

A Powerful Culture Starts with You

Into the second year of the COVID-19 pandemic, as I started giving talks to leaders again, I asked them to share what mindsets were empowering them to get through this difficult time when work was remote, shipments were delayed, customers were unsure about the products and services they wanted and there was a general sense of ambivalence and malaise about when this pandemic might "end."

The words I heard over and over again were *agility, openness, seeking feedback, caring about our team* and *getting creative.* Across industries, leaders had an intention that they were going to make it and prosper in the process. They may not have realized it at the time, but somewhere along the way, they made a declaration that they would succeed.

On the personal side, some lost weight, tended to hobbies and spent more time with their families. All things from the Esteem Portfolio that expanded and enriched their lives and their confidence. "I've gained two hours a day in commute time that I'm able to spend with my family and toward my self-development," I heard repeatedly.

This longing for extra hours of personal time drove many people, whose companies returned to in-person office work again, to seek other employment. Part of keeping the best employees is learning what their needs are and doing your best to meet them. The companies that were most agile were able to retain more of their staff. The pandemic has taught leaders and employees alike that work can continue, even when there is more flexibility.

As we conclude this book, I ask you the same questions that I ask at the end of a coaching session:

- What have you learned about yourself?
- What new actions might you take?
- What mindset did you have when you started this book and how has your thinking evolved?

As you take steps to refine your culture, know that seeking feedback takes courage. Deciding to implement new actions is bold. Remember, *Petit a petit l'oiseu fait son nid.* Bit by bit, the bird builds its nest. When it comes to strengthening your leadership, your team and your company, remember that you create change by taking one step at a time, one day at a time. You are planting seeds, watering and nurturing them. One day, when you least expect it, at a team meeting or in a conversation, an employee will say something about your company's culture that will, like a mirror, reflect who you are and what you have been doing. You may hear comments such as:

- "We need to keep this decision in line with our strategy."
- "That person is behaving outside of our values."
- "We need to be seeking input from our people."
- "How will this decision impact our culture?"

You will get back from yourself in proportion to what you invest in yourself. You will get out of your company what you put into it.

Here's to your wisdom, power, resilience and grace! Here's to your creating the team and company of your dreams!

A Powerful Culture Starts with You!